STEPHEN HAWKING
A LIFE BEYOND LIMITS

Neil Armstrong

Jackie Robinson

Harriet Tubman

Jane Goodall

Beyoncé

Albert Einstein

Stephen Hawking

Simone Biles

≫TRAIL BLAZERS

STEPHEN HAWKING
A LIFE BEYOND LIMITS

ALEX WOOLF

RANDOM HOUSE 🏠 NEW YORK

Text copyright © 2020 by Alex Woolf
Cover art copyright © 2020 by Luisa Uribe
Interior illustrations copyright © 2020 by David Shephard
Additional images used under license from Shutterstock.com

All rights reserved. Published in the United States by Random House Children's Books, a division of Penguin Random House LLC, New York.

Random House and the colophon are registered trademarks of Penguin Random House LLC.

Visit us on the Web! rhcbooks.com

Educators and librarians, for a variety of teaching tools, visit us at RHTeachersLibrarians.com

Library of Congress Cataloging-in-Publication Data
Name: Woolf, Alex, author.
Title: Stephen Hawking: a life beyond limits / Alex Woolf.
Description: New York: Random House Children's Books, 2020 |
Series: Trailblazers | Includes bibliographical references and index.
Identifiers: LCCN 2019046807 | ISBN 978-0-593-12449-9 (trade pbk.) |
ISBN 978-0-593-12450-5 (lib. bdg.) | ISBN 978-0-593-12451-2 (ebook)
Subjects: LCSH: Hawking, Stephen, 1942–2018—Juvenile literature. |
Physicists—Great Britain—Biography—Juvenile literature. |
Amyotrophic lateral sclerosis—Patients—Great Britain—
Biography—Juvenile literature.
Classification: LCC QC16.H33 W66 2020 | DDC 530/.092 [B]—dc23

Created by Stripes Publishing Limited, an imprint of the Little Tiger Group

Printed in the United States of America

10 9 8 7 6 5 4 3 2 1
First Edition

Random House Children's Books supports the First Amendment and celebrates the right to read.

Contents

Introduction — 1
Black Holes Ain't So Black

Chapter 1 — 11
Early Promise

Chapter 2 — 29
Studying the Cosmos

Chapter 3 — 55
A Great Discovery

Chapter 4 — 73
Growing Fame

Chapter 5 — 87
A Brief History of Time

Chapter 6 — 107
New Theories

Chapter 7 — 123
Not Slowing Down

Conclusion — 141
Asking the Big Questions

Timeline — 152

Further Reading — 156

Glossary — 158

Index — 164

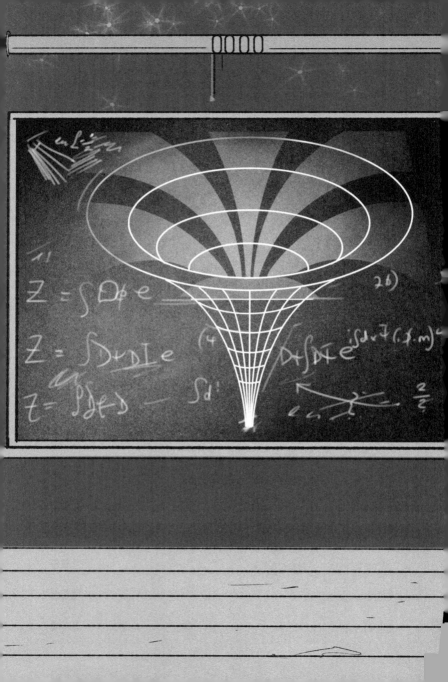

INTRODUCTION

BLACK HOLES AIN'T SO BLACK

In 1974, an English physicist made an incredible discovery about the most mysterious regions of space—black holes. Before Stephen Hawking began studying them, scientists had believed that black holes were like graves: things went into them, but nothing ever came out! Using mathematics, Stephen figured out that this was wrong. Black holes actually glow. They give off radiation. It seemed astonishing at the time—and it still does—that anything could come out of a black hole, which is like an enormously powerful vacuum cleaner in space. Other scientists checked Stephen's calculations and were forced to admit he was right. He had made one of the most significant breakthroughs of the twentieth century and changed the way we look at the universe forever. As Stephen once put it:

Black holes ain't so black.

He would go on to make many more discoveries, becoming a leading figure in the field of cosmology and one of the most famous scientists in the world.

WHAT ARE BLACK HOLES?

Imagine a star bigger than our sun being squeezed to the size of a tiny point—a point so small, it can't even be measured. Think how dense that point would be, with all that matter crushed inside it. If a star collapsed to something that tiny, you might expect it to have dramatic consequences, and you'd be right: the gravity it would generate would be so powerful, it would suck in everything around it. Even light wouldn't be able to escape its pull.

If this seems impossible, think again. It happens. The crushed stars are called black holes, and there are millions of them in the universe right now. There's even one at the heart of our galaxy. Don't be scared, though. The closest one to Earth is three thousand light-years away, so we're well out of the danger zone!

Scientists had been speculating about the possibility of black holes for more than two hundred years, but it wasn't until 1972 that one was actually detected. Even then, these objects remained mystifying, until Stephen Hawking unraveled many of their secrets.

Observing Black Holes

Since light is unable to escape from black holes, they cannot be observed directly. Astronomers searching for them must look for indirect evidence of their presence—for example, by detecting their gravitational effect on nearby objects. The first actual image of a black hole was released in April 2019. It looked like a glowing doughnut! What it showed was the accretion disc, a bright ring of gas and dust getting sucked into the black hole in the center.

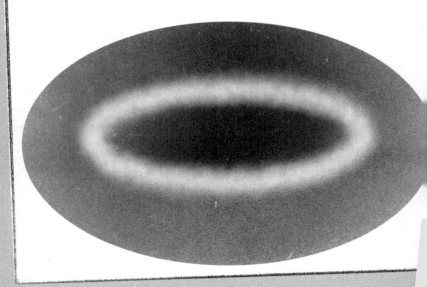

FROM DARK STARS TO BLACK HOLES

Scientists have been looking to the skies for centuries, trying to solve the mysteries of the cosmos. In 1783, an English clergyman and amateur scientist named John Michell suggested that the surface gravity of some stars might be so strong that light can't escape from them. He called these bodies "dark stars" and thought the universe might be full of them, all invisible to our eyes.

More than a century later, in 1915, German physicist Albert Einstein introduced his theory of general relativity. His equations showed that gravity is actually a warping of space-time caused by objects with mass. The more massive the object, the more it warps space-time.

Space-Time

Space-time is time plus three-dimensional space viewed as a four-dimensional thing. It's difficult for us to visualize this with our three-dimensional brains, but it's a useful way for physicists to view the cosmos.

One way of thinking of space-time is as a stretchy rubber sheet that warps when something with mass (like Earth) is placed on it.

Then German astronomer and military officer Karl Schwarzschild used Einstein's equations to make a startling discovery: he realized that a massive object squeezed into a small enough space would produce such a powerful gravitational field that nothing could escape from it, not even light. Schwarzschild calculated that if anything gets within a certain distance of such an object, it becomes trapped by it, and escape is impossible. This distance, marking the point of no return, became known as the "event horizon." The event horizon is so called because it describes a line beyond which, like a horizon, you cannot see. For example, if a flashlight were to fall inside an event horizon, no one outside would ever see its light.

Neither Einstein nor Schwarzschild believed that dark stars actually existed. However, as the twentieth century progressed and astronomers learned more about the life cycles of stars, dark stars became ever more conceivable.

Scientists learned that a star's gravity is always trying to pull its mass inward. This is balanced by the outward pressure exerted by the burning of the star's nuclear fuel. But at the end of a star's life, when it runs out of fuel, its gravity will cause it to collapse. In 1939, American physicist J. Robert Oppenheimer showed that a star with enough mass will have sufficient gravity to collapse to a single point of infinite density and gravity, known as a singularity. In other words, it will become a dark star.

During the 1960s, astronomers started discovering massive, extremely remote celestial objects called quasars, which could only be explained by the presence of a dark star. Scientists were starting to accept that these might be real. By 1964, some science journalists had taken to calling dark stars "black holes," and the term was then popularized by American physicist John Wheeler in 1967.

quasar

⋛ A BREAKTHROUGH SCIENTIST ⋚

It was around this time that a young Stephen Hawking began studying black holes and the singularity that lies at their heart. While Stephen was doing his pioneering research on black holes, he was also coping with a major personal challenge.

In his early twenties, he was diagnosed with a rare and terrible disease. The disease attacked the nerves controlling his muscles, gradually paralyzing him. He was told he would have just a few years to live.

Nevertheless, he remained determined to pursue his research and lead a full and active life. Thanks to the love and support of his family, along with the assistance of some cutting-edge technology, he was able to do so.

In addition to his discoveries about black holes, Stephen made major contributions to our understanding of the cosmos and how the universe began. He also wrote the bestselling book *A Brief History of Time*, in which he explained the latest discoveries about the universe in language that ordinary readers could understand.

Throughout his life, Stephen Hawking refused to be limited by his disability. In this, as well as in his scientific achievements, he was a true trailblazer.

However bad life may seem, there is always something you can do and succeed at.

CHAPTER 1
EARLY PROMISE

Stephen William Hawking was born in Oxford, England, on January 8, 1942, exactly three hundred years after the death of the great Italian astronomer and physicist Galileo. Like Galileo, Stephen would grow up to make important discoveries about the universe.

When Stephen was born, World War II was raging, and British cities were suffering frequent air raids from German bombers. Stephen's parents, Frank and Isobel, lived in Highgate, North London. Hardly a night passed without the sound of bombs exploding, and they decided it would be safer to go to Oxford for Stephen's birth.

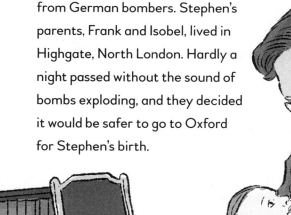

During the war, the Germans did not bomb Oxford. Britain's other great university town, Cambridge, escaped with very light bombing. There was a rumor at the time that this was because of an agreement between the Germans and the British not to bomb each other's most important university towns. However, there is no evidence that such an agreement was ever made.

Family Background

Stephen's father came from a family of farmers. His grandfather went bankrupt, and his grandmother saved the family from ruin by opening a school in their home. This enabled them to send young Frank, Stephen's father, to Oxford University. Frank went on to become an expert in tropical medicine. Stephen's mother was the daughter of a Scottish doctor, the third of eight children. Like Frank's family, hers wasn't wealthy, but they managed to send Isobel to Oxford. After graduating, she did several jobs before becoming a secretary in a medical research institute, where she met Frank.

ROCKET ATTACK

Frank's job was in London, so shortly after Stephen was born, the family returned to Highgate. In November 1944, a German V-2 rocket landed on a house just a few doors away from Stephen's. The blast blew out the back windows of the Hawkings' home, sending glass shards into the opposite wall. Frank was home at the time, but luckily he wasn't hurt. For years after the blast, young Stephen played in the large bomb site with his neighborhood friend Howard.

Stephen was Frank and Isobel's eldest child. After him, they had two daughters, Mary and Philippa. Stephen attended Byron House School in Highgate. This was a progressive school with some unusual teaching methods. The teachers didn't believe in making children learn through repetition and memorization, which was the common method in schools at the time. Instead, children were supposed to work independently at their own pace, and learn without realizing it. Stephen complained to his parents that the school wasn't teaching him anything. He blamed this for the fact that he didn't learn to read until he was eight. His sister Philippa went to a more conventional school and could read by the age of four.

But then Philippa was definitely brighter than me.

MODEL TRAINS

Frank and Isobel believed strongly in the importance of education. Frank taught his children astronomy, and Isobel often took them to visit museums in London. Mary's favorite was the Natural History Museum, while Stephen preferred the Science Museum. Isobel would leave the older children on their own to explore their favorite exhibitions while she took Philippa to the Victoria and Albert Museum.

As a child, Stephen loved model trains. Toys weren't made during the war, because the toy factories were turned to weapon production, so Frank Hawking built his son a wooden train set. When Stephen asked for a train that moved on its own, Frank found a secondhand wind-up train, which he repaired and gave to Stephen for Christmas. After the war, Frank went to the United States, where he bought a model train with a cowcatcher—a metal grille for pushing large objects off the track in front of a train—and a figure-eight track. Stephen was overjoyed with this and played with it constantly.

When he was older, Stephen built model airplanes and boats. These were rickety constructions of balsa wood and paper. They rarely flew or sailed very well. Stephen was never much good with his hands, but he had help from his best friend at school, John McClenahan, who was better coordinated than he was. Stephen's aim was to build something he could control. Later in his life, Stephen would build scientific models using a computer to explain his theories about the universe.

Scientific Models

A scientific model is a simplified representation of something in the real world—usually a complex, changing thing, such as a city, the earth's climate, or even the universe itself. Scientists build models by taking known data and combining this with mathematics and logic. They use models to try to understand or visualize a complex, real-world thing. Models can also help scientists predict what might happen in the future, or how actions they take could affect the thing they are modeling.

AN ECCENTRIC FAMILY

In 1950, when Stephen was eight, Frank Hawking got a new job, and the family moved to St. Albans, a city just to the north of London. Here, they bought a large, elegant, rather ramshackle house.

The family car was a converted London taxi. Frank installed a table in the back so that the children could play cards and games during long journeys. They spent their vacations in a painted wooden trailer in Dorset, close to the beach. Stephen's friend John McClenahan would often join them there. Together, the boys flew kites, ate ice cream, and thought up new ways to tease Mary and Philippa.

The Hawking family also loved reading and had hundreds of books placed two deep on their shelves. Meals were often spent with each person silently reading. When the Hawkings did speak, they did so extremely quickly, and often in a family dialect that other people found hard to understand. Friends called it "Hawkingese." There was no central heating, and broken windows weren't replaced. As a result, the house could be freezing in the winter.

The books provided some insulation!

The Hawkings were a highly intelligent family, but also known to be quite eccentric. Visitors arrived at the house to the sound of opera being played at loud volume, or they might hear the buzzing of the bees that Frank kept in the cellar. Occasionally, Stephen's grandmother would descend from her attic room to play the piano.

⋛ STARTING SCHOOL ⋛

Upon the family's arrival at St. Albans, Stephen's parents sent him to the High School for Girls, which, in spite of its name, admitted boys up to age ten. Stephen only stayed there a few months. That winter, his father had to make a long trip to Africa. Isobel didn't want to be left alone, so she took the children to the Spanish island of Majorca, where they stayed with Isobel's university friend Beryl and her husband, the famous author Robert Graves. They had a blissful time in the Mediterranean, and a tutor was hired for Stephen so he could continue with his studies.

The family returned to England, and when Stephen was ten, he passed a test to get into the exclusive St. Albans School. He was a bright boy, but quite lazy. His classwork was messy, and his handwriting made teachers despair. In his first year at St. Albans, he was ranked third from the bottom of his class. This was partly because he found subjects like math and science very easy and didn't bother to apply himself. As for subjects like English literature, he decided he had no need for them.

Instead, Stephen devoted his energies to other kinds of activity. He enjoyed music, drama, ballroom dancing, cross-country running, and tennis (though he played it badly). He had a sense of fun, enjoyed practical jokes, and excelled at slow bicycle racing.

Despite his low grades, both teachers and pupils saw there was something special about Stephen. He was always questioning how things worked, from clocks and radios to the universe. His friends called him "Einstein."

Albert Einstein

Stephen's friends nicknamed him "Einstein," because he reminded them of the brilliant and eccentric scientist Albert Einstein (1879—1955). During his life, Einstein published numerous papers that would transform our understanding of the universe. One of them contained the famous equation $E = mc^2$, which states that matter can be converted into energy. In 1915, Einstein presented his theory of general relativity. This theory would play a key role in Stephen Hawking's later discoveries about black holes.

Frank and Isobel had high hopes for Stephen. When he turned thirteen, they planned for him to go to Westminster, an even more prestigious school than St. Albans. They couldn't afford the fees but hoped Stephen would win a scholarship. Unfortunately, on the day of the scholarship exam, Stephen fell ill with mononucleosis and had to stay home in bed.

Although his parents' hopes were dashed, Stephen was happy enough to continue at St. Alban's, where he had formed a close circle of friends. As well as building models, they made fireworks and played complicated board games that Stephen invented. Some of these games were so complex that it could take them hours to discuss the consequences of a single throw of the dice.

Frank and Isobel adopted a son, Edward, when Stephen was fourteen. Stephen was very accepting of the new addition to the family. He said later that Edward "was probably good for us. He was a rather difficult child, but one couldn't help liking him."

When Stephen was fifteen, he read in a book that the universe was expanding. This bothered him, since he realized that if it continued to expand, it would eventually become almost completely empty.

An Expanding Universe

In 1929, American astronomer Edwin Hubble (1889—1953) proved that there is a relationship between the speed of distant galaxies and their distance from our own galaxy. The best way to imagine the expansion is not as galaxies rushing away from each other but as the space between them swelling. Think of the universe as a loaf of raisin bread dough expanding in the oven: the raisins (galaxies) move away from each other, but they're still inside the dough.

The most ambitious project Stephen and his friends undertook was to build their own computer. This was quite an achievement in the 1950s, which was not long after the first computers had been invented. They were helped by their math teacher, Mr. Tahta. They called it LUCE (Logical Uniselector Computing Engine) and built it out of recycled parts from clocks and other mechanical devices, including an old telephone switchboard. LUCE could perform simple mathematical calculations.

INDIAN ADVENTURE

In 1959, Frank had to go on a research project to India. Isobel decided to accompany him, taking the younger children with her. Stephen remained in England so he could take important school tests and university entrance exams. He stayed with the family of Dr. John Humphrey, a colleague of Frank's, at their house in Mill Hill, London. During the summer break, Stephen joined his family in Lucknow, India. He was looking forward to trying some Indian cuisine, but his father refused to eat it. Frank had employed an ex-British Army cook to serve English food.

Stephen had many adventures while in India. On one expedition into the mountains of Kashmir, the Hawkings got caught in monsoon floods, and their car, which they'd brought from England, had to be towed to safety by a local truck driver.

This wouldn't happen in St. Albans.

WHAT TO STUDY?

As Stephen entered his final year in school, his thoughts turned to what subject he should study at university and which college he should apply to. Oxford and Cambridge Universities are made up of colleges, which are like self-contained communities. Each college has its own departments, teaching staff, and residence halls. Frank wanted his son to study medicine at University College, Oxford, as he had done. However, medicine involves an understanding of biology, and Stephen wasn't all that interested in biology. He preferred physics, because it looks at more fundamental things, like the forces that hold atoms together and keep planets rotating around stars. Even more than physics, Stephen loved mathematics. This was thanks in part to his inspiring teacher Mr. Tahta. Frank pointed out that there weren't many jobs for mathematicians besides teaching.

Also, mathematics wasn't taught at University College.

Stephen decided to follow his father's advice—up to a point. He wouldn't go into medicine, but he applied to University College to study physics and chemistry. Both Stephen's headmaster at St. Albans and his father were worried that Stephen didn't have what it took to win a scholarship to Oxford. His grades were average, and he was ranked no higher than halfway up his class. The headmaster suggested he wait another year before applying. But they both underestimated Stephen's abilities. When he took the entrance exam in March 1959, he achieved near-perfect marks in the physics section, and he performed extremely well in the interview. At the age of seventeen, Stephen was awarded a scholarship to study natural science with an emphasis on physics at University College.

CHAPTER 2
STUDYING THE COSMOS

Stephen entered University College, Oxford, in October 1959. He was one of only four physics students to enter Univ (as the college was known) that term. The other three were Gordon Berry, Richard Bryan, and Derek Powney. They quickly formed a clique and spent most of their time together. Stephen was particularly close to Gordon Berry, who was his partner during tutorials, which are teaching sessions that include a teacher and a very small group of students.

University College, Oxford

University College, nicknamed Univ, was founded in 1249, making it one of the oldest Oxford colleges. Famous alumni include Stephen Hawking; former US president Bill Clinton; writer C. S. Lewis; poet Percy Bysshe Shelley; and two British prime ministers, Clement Attlee and Harold Wilson.

ANYTHING BUT GRAY

Stephen didn't enjoy Oxford much at first. Apart from Gordon, Richard, and Derek, he made no friends and felt quite isolated and lonely. Most of the students in his year were older than he was, partly because he had taken his exams a year early, but also because they had done National Service. From 1949 to 1960, all healthy men ages eighteen to twenty-one were expected to serve in the armed forces for eighteen months. Mandatory service was abolished just as Stephen turned eighteen.

For some students, a poor social life might have meant more time for studying, but not for Stephen. Since his early school days, he had realized he could get reasonable marks by hardly trying at all, and he continued this pattern of behavior at university. He wasn't the only one to take this attitude. At that time in Oxford, according to Stephen, you were supposed to be either effortlessly brilliant or content to get a fourth-class degree. This was the lowest degree you could get without actually failing.

British Degree System

During the time that Stephen Hawking attended university, the degrees that students could achieve were:

FIRST-CLASS HONORS	85%+
SECOND-CLASS HONORS	70—85%
THIRD-CLASS HONORS	55—70%
FOURTH-CLASS HONORS	40—55%

In the 1970s, this system was changed so that second class and third class became upper second and lower second, and fourth class became third class.

The one thing you weren't supposed to do was work hard. This marked you as a "gray man" (a dull person), which was frowned upon.

⋛ BRILLIANT BUT LAZY ⋚

Students taking the three-year physics course at Oxford didn't have exams until the end of their final year, so there was little pressure on them. Stephen didn't bother attending lectures and went to just one or two tutorials a week. He and Gordon avoided spending time in the laboratory by faking parts of their experiments and finding other ways to obtain data. Stephen later calculated he spent, on average, just one hour a day studying, adding up to a thousand hours over three years. Stephen's laziness did not go completely unnoticed. One tutor commented that Stephen preferred finding mistakes in the textbooks to solving the problems.

I'm not proud of this lack of work. This was just the way I was at the time.

Part of the reason why Stephen was able to get away with doing so little work was his extraordinary intelligence. On one occasion, his tutor Robert Berman handed Stephen and his friends an assignment on electricity and magnetism. He gave them thirteen extremely difficult problems and told them to solve as many as they could by the following week's tutorial. By the end of the week, Gordon had solved just one of the problems, while Richard and Derek had managed one and a half. Stephen had not even begun working on them. The tutorial was in the afternoon, so he skipped three morning lectures to study the problems. When he met up with his friends at noon, he admitted gloomily that he had only been able to solve ten. At first they thought he was joking, but then they looked at his work and saw that it was true. That was the moment, according to Derek, when they realized that Stephen was a genius.

> "It was not just that we weren't in the same street [as Stephen], we weren't on the same planet."
> —Derek Powney

Berman was also quick to realize Stephen's brilliance: "Undergraduate physics was simply not a challenge for him. He did very little work, really, because anything that was doable, he could do. . . . I'm not conceited enough to think that I ever taught him anything."

⇒ RECKLESS ON THE RIVER ⇐

Halfway through his second year at Oxford, Stephen decided to make more of an effort to get involved in university life and joined the college boat club. He had no interest in being a rower—he didn't have the physique for it. He wanted to be a coxswain—the person who sits at the back of the boat looking forward, guiding the rowers (who face backward) with his voice and steering the boat with the rudder. Stephen was ideally suited to this role, being lightly built and quick-minded, with a loud, commanding voice. He enjoyed the feeling of being in control of the boat in much the same way as he had enjoyed controlling model boats and trains when he was younger.

As a coxswain, Stephen soon gained a reputation for being reckless, steering his crew on risky maneuvers that often ended in collisions, broken oars, and damaged boats. Norman Dix, whose job was to take care of the boats, recalled Stephen as an "adventurous type; you never knew quite what he was going to do." Stephen described his rowing career as "fairly disastrous." In his first race, his boat was disqualified for going off course. In a later race, he was involved in a head-on collision with another boat.

Stephen made lots of friends in the boat club and, as a result, was much happier during this period at Oxford. He emerged from his shell of isolation to become a popular figure around the college. He was known for his independent spirit, quick wit, long hair, and love of classical music and science fiction.

FINAL EXAMS

One thing Stephen was still not known for, however, was hard work—he put more effort into his rowing than into his studies. So when he reached the end of his third year, and the time came for him to take his final exams, he was woefully ill prepared. This was a problem because Stephen had his heart set on continuing his academic career after completing his degree. He wanted to work as a graduate student at Cambridge University, doing research for a PhD, a degree awarded to students who complete a thesis that offers a significant new contribution to knowledge in their subject. To do that, Stephen would need to get a first-class degree, the highest grade of academic achievement.

The final exams consisted of many questions—far more than anyone could be expected to answer. Stephen calculated that his best hope lay in answering only the theoretical questions and ignoring the ones that required a knowledge of facts. He wasn't at all confident that his strategy would work, but having done so little studying, he had no choice. As a fallback plan, he had applied to join the civil service, where he would work as an administrator in a government department. Despite not really preparing for it, he passed the interview for the civil service. The next stage was a written exam.

The night before his Oxford finals, Stephen was so nervous he couldn't sleep. Because of this, he didn't perform as well as he could have. All was not lost, however. He could still join the civil service, providing he passed the written exam. Unfortunately, he overslept and missed it. Now everything depended on the results of his finals!

Stephen and his friends waited nervously for the results of their exams. Gordon and Derek got seconds. Richard, disappointingly, got a third. Stephen was on the borderline between a first and a second. To make their final judgment on his result, the examiners summoned Stephen for a *viva voce*, or oral exam. They asked him about his future plans. Stephen knew he had a reputation as a difficult student and tried to work this to his advantage. "If I get a first, I shall go to Cambridge," he said. "If I receive a second, I will remain at Oxford, so I expect you will give me a first." They duly awarded him a first.

> "[The examiners] were intelligent enough to realize they were talking to someone far cleverer than most of themselves."
> —Dr. Robert Berman

SOMETHING AMISS

Stephen's final year at Oxford had been very busy, what with the boat club, his flourishing social life, and exam worries, yet he couldn't fail to ignore that something was wrong with his health. He was getting clumsy, and sometimes he fell for no apparent reason. On trips on the river in a one-man boat, he struggled to use the oars. During his final term, he fell down the stairs and landed on his head, resulting in a temporary loss of memory. He went to see a doctor, but tests showed no brain damage.

In the summer following his finals in 1962, Stephen and a friend, John Elder, went on a trip to Persia (now Iran). In the capital, Tehran, they parted company, and

Stephen continued his journey with another student, Richard Chiin. They went south to Isfahan, Shiraz, and Persepolis, the ancient capital. From there, they crossed the desert to Mashhad. During their return journey, Stephen became seriously ill from dysentery, an infection of the intestines. Neither of them noticed when their bus drove through a major earthquake. In his distressed state, Stephen thought the bus was just driving too fast on a very bumpy road! Because Stephen and Richard didn't understand the Iranian language, they didn't find out about the disaster until several days later.

Buin Zahra Earthquake

The earthquake took place in Buin Zahra, Qazvin Province, Iran, at 10:50 p.m. on September 1, 1962. It was classified as a major earthquake, with a Richter magnitude of 7.1. At least 12,225 people were killed, and 2,776 were injured. More than 21,000 houses were destroyed in nearby villages.

CAMBRIDGE

Due to his mysterious clumsiness and his illness in Persia, Stephen arrived in Cambridge in the autumn of 1962 feeling physically weakened. Nevertheless, he was excited to be getting started on his graduate work. He had decided to specialize in a branch of theoretical physics called cosmology. He was attracted to cosmology because it asked big, fundamental questions, like how the universe came into existence and how it would end. In 1929, astronomer Edwin Hubble (see page 23) discovered that the universe was expanding. Cosmologists disagreed about what this meant, and the debate was still going on when Stephen arrived at Cambridge. The main two competing models were the "big bang" and "steady state" theories.

FRED HOYLE

One of the main reasons Stephen had applied to study cosmology at Cambridge was the chance to work with the great astronomer Fred Hoyle, co-inventor of the steady state theory. When Stephen arrived, he was therefore bitterly disappointed to discover that Hoyle had enough students already. Instead, Stephen was assigned to Dennis Sciama, who was much less well known—in fact, Stephen hadn't heard of him before. It turned out for the best, however, because Hoyle was a busy man who was hardly ever around, whereas Sciama proved to be an excellent mentor for Stephen.

DENNIS SCIAMA

Big Bang Theory

According to the big bang theory, the universe has not always existed. It began with a singularity before expanding and cooling to form the universe of today. The theory explains why the galaxies are moving away from us and why the speed at which they move away is dependent on their distance. By analyzing the expansion rate of the universe, scientists have calculated that the big bang happened around 13.8 billion years ago. Today, we can detect leftover radiation (energy) from the big bang in the form of something called cosmic microwave background radiation (CMBR). The term "big bang" was invented by Fred Hoyle, a supporter of the "steady state" model, as a way of belittling the rival theory.

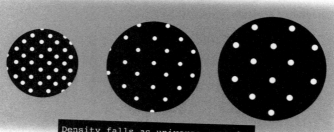

Density falls as universe expands.

Steady State Theory

This theory proposes that the universe has always existed and has no beginning or end. The universe is expanding, but its average density never changes, because new matter is constantly being created, eventually forming new stars and galaxies to fill up the gaps. The theory was put forward in 1948 by British scientists Hermann Bondi, Thomas Gold, and Fred Hoyle. Steady state would eventually lose out to the big bang theory as a model to describe the universe. The discovery of CMBR in 1964 contradicted the steady state model and led almost all scientists to accept the big bang theory. However, when Stephen Hawking arrived at Cambridge in 1962, the debate was still very much alive.

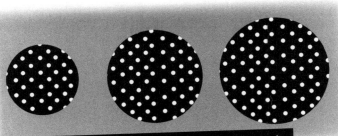

Density stays the same as universe expands.

≡ DEVASTATING NEWS ≡

During Stephen's first term at Cambridge, his clumsiness kept getting worse. He struggled to tie his shoes and sometimes slurred his words. During the Christmas break, when skating on a lake in St. Albans, he fell and couldn't get up.

His parents took him to see the family doctor, who referred him to a specialist. In January 1963, shortly after his twenty-first birthday, Stephen headed up to St. Bartholomew's Hospital in London, where doctors performed various tests on him. They gave him some devastating news. Stephen had a rare and incurable disease: amyotrophic lateral sclerosis (ALS), also known as Lou Gehrig's disease.

Amyotrophic Lateral Sclerosis

ALS gradually destroys the nerve cells in the spinal cord and brain that control the body's muscles. It doesn't affect all the muscles, only the voluntary ones—the ones used for movement. Involuntary muscles, such as those of the heart and lungs, are unaffected. Other organs, such as the brain, are also unaffected. As the nerve cells die, the muscles they control waste away, so movement and speech become impossible. At the time when Stephen Hawking was diagnosed, death usually occurred within two to five years, with most people dying within 14 months of being diagnosed. Thanks to recent medical advances, around 20 percent of people with ALS live five years or more after diagnosis, and about 10 percent live more than 10 years. Stephen Hawking was the longest-living survivor of ALS.

Lou Gehrig (1903—1941) was a renowned baseball player for the New York Yankees during the 1920s and 1930s. In 1939, he was forced to retire after being diagnosed with ALS, and he died two years later. ALS is commonly referred to as Lou Gehrig's disease.

For Stephen, the discovery that he had this disease came as a terrible shock. He felt angry and frustrated that his life would be cut short when there was so much he wanted to do. It seemed pointless to continue working toward his PhD when he probably wouldn't live to receive it. But this feeling of despair was softened by something he had witnessed while in the hospital: in the bed opposite him, he had seen a boy die of leukemia. He understood that no matter how bad he felt, there were people in even worse situations.

Whenever I feel inclined to be sorry for myself, I remember that boy.

Stephen began having disturbing dreams about dying. They made him realize that there were still things he wanted to do with his life, and if he was going to die soon, he'd better get on with doing them. Up until that point, he had always done his best to avoid work and put little effort into his studies. He no longer wanted to live that way—not when every year or month might be his last.

JANE WILDE

Soon Stephen would have another reason for embracing life. He first met Jane Wilde at a party in St. Albans in January 1963, before he was in the hospital. Jane was in her last year at St. Albans High School and had been accepted by London University to study languages. In her memoir, *Travelling to Infinity: My Life With Stephen,* she recalled him as "slight of frame ... gesticulating with long thin fingers as he spoke—his hair falling across his face over his glasses." She liked his intelligence and self-mocking wit. They exchanged contact details. A few days later, he invited her to his twenty-first birthday party, and Jane got her first experience of Stephen's eccentric family and their drafty, ramshackle house.

Stephen adored Jane and wanted to impress her. He took her on dates to the theater and the opera, and to his college's May Ball—an unforgettable night of music and dancing, where festivities continued until dawn. Jane quickly realized that Stephen had physical problems. He had trouble pouring drinks, for example. But she had no idea how serious his condition was. When she asked him about it, she could see it made him uncomfortable, so she dropped the subject.

FIRST ADVENTURE

On one of their early dates, Stephen treated Jane to an expensive trip to a restaurant and the theater in London. As they were boarding the bus on the way home, Stephen realized he didn't have enough money for the fare. Sheepishly, he asked if Jane wouldn't mind paying. But Jane had left her purse at the theater! So they jumped off the bus and sneaked back into the theater through the stage door. Jane found her purse under her seat. But then the lights went out. In pitch darkness, Stephen took her hand and led her back to the exit.

By the end of 1963, Jane and Stephen were in love, but Jane was also scared. She wanted to spend her life with him, but Stephen was quite clear that they wouldn't have very long together. Beyond that, he didn't like to discuss his illness. In the autumn of 1963, Stephen proposed to Jane, and she accepted. Students at Jane's college weren't normally allowed to get married, but a special exception was made because of the groom's life expectancy. Stephen and Jane were married on July 14, 1965, and then went for a weeklong honeymoon in Suffolk.

> The engagement changed my life. It gave me something to live for. It made me determined to live.

CHALLENGING FRED HOYLE

Not knowing how much time he had left, Stephen threw himself into his studies. He shared an office in the physics department at Cambridge with Jayant Narlikar, a former student of Fred Hoyle's. Jayant was helping Hoyle look at ways of explaining new discoveries in astronomy that were casting doubt on a steady state universe. Stephen was intrigued and began looking in more detail at Jayant's work.

In June 1964, Stephen attended a lecture given by Fred Hoyle on this subject. At the end, Fred called for questions. Stephen rose to his feet with difficulty and challenged one of Fred's results. Fred was astonished and asked Stephen how he could possibly know that the result was wrong. Stephen replied that he had "worked it out." Fred and the audience assumed Stephen meant he'd figured it out in his head during the lecture—in fact, he'd calculated it before the meeting, by looking at Jayant's work. The audience was impressed, but Fred was furious. Stephen was already making his mark as a bold and brilliant young physicist.

⋛ COLLAPSING STARS ⋚

For his thesis, Stephen chose to focus on something discovered by British mathematician and physicist Roger Penrose. Scientists already knew that when a star has no more fuel left to burn, it will collapse under the force of its own gravity. Einstein's equations proved that a perfectly spherical star would collapse all the way down to a single point of infinite density called a singularity. What Penrose showed was that this could happen to any star, not just perfectly spherical ones, which don't exist in nature. Stephen took up this idea and imagined that time was reversed, so a singularity exploded outward and kept expanding. That, he suggested, could be an explanation for the big bang. With Dennis Sciama's encouragement, Stephen decided to make this the subject of his PhD. He worked on his idea until he was able to prove it mathematically.

Stephen needed to support himself financially while he worked on his PhD. In 1965, he applied for a Cambridge research fellowship, which is a paid position for academics at a university involving research and often some teaching. Jane helped him write the application. He needed to name two people as referees—people willing to say in writing that Stephen was of good character and ability. He named Dennis Sciama and the famous cosmologist Hermann Bondi, whom he knew a little and who had previously agreed to write him a reference. Unfortunately, when the university wrote to Hermann, he replied that he didn't know Stephen. He'd forgotten they'd ever met! This could have ruined Stephen's chances of an academic career, but Dennis Sciama immediately wrote to Hermann, reminding him that he had met Stephen. Hermann then wrote him a glowing reference, and Stephen was granted the research fellowship.

By now, Stephen walked with a cane and slurred his words, but his condition seemed to have stabilized. Having married Jane, and with his career going well, he could start to look with a little more hope to the future.

CHAPTER 3

A GREAT DISCOVERY

In October 1965, Stephen began his research fellowship at Cambridge. He and Jane rented a small cottage in Little St. Mary's Lane, just down the road from the Department of Applied Mathematics and Theoretical Physics (DAMTP), where he would be working. In March 1966, Stephen's thesis was approved, and he and Jane could celebrate the completion of his PhD. Not only that, he was that year's joint winner (with Roger Penrose) of the prestigious Adams Prize for an essay he wrote on singularities.

⋛ LEARNING TO COPE ⋛

By the fall, Stephen's fingers were beginning to curl, and he could no longer write. Soon, he couldn't move around without crutches, and by 1970 he was forced to use a wheelchair. Yet he refused to surrender to his disability. He would spend fifteen minutes climbing up the stairs to his bedroom, insisting on doing it without help. He joked that it gave him extra thinking time.

One trait Stephen never lost was his sense of humor and his willingness to make light of himself. Dennis Sciama used to say that it was more important to go to coffee than to go to seminars, and Stephen followed this advice. He made a point of talking to colleagues informally during coffee breaks. This made him very popular with his fellow researchers at DAMTP, who might otherwise have been too awed by his intelligence or discomfited by his disability to approach him.

≡ BECOMING A DAD ≡

The Hawkings' first child, Robert, was born in May 1967. A daughter, Lucy, followed in November 1970; and their third and final child, Timothy, was born in April 1979. Having children gave Stephen a new lease on life, but it was also frustrating for him that he couldn't play with them in an energetic way, like other fathers.

He tried to be as active as possible, though. Robert has memories of him and his sister playing chase with their father in their back garden when they were little. Stephen took them to car races and waterslide parks. He supported Robert's interest in computers and always made a point of going to see Lucy in her school plays. Even so, the children knew that their father was not like most dads. They saw up close every day that he needed help doing the simplest tasks.

Stephen and Jane successfully campaigned for wheelchair access at DAMTP and at the theaters and opera houses he loved to visit in London. But Jane was struggling to bear all the responsibilities of home and family. She tried to persuade Stephen to accept a live-in caregiver. At first he refused, but in 1974, she convinced him to accept a new arrangement. They took in one of Stephen's graduate students, Bernard Carr. In exchange for free accommodation and getting help from Stephen with his studies, Bernard would assist him in getting into bed and getting up.

NEW WAYS OF THINKING

As he lost his ability to write, Stephen began to train his mind to think in a different way. He did mathematical calculations in his head by forming mental pictures. "Equations," said Stephen, "are just the boring part of mathematics. I prefer to see things in terms of geometry." One physicist, Werner Israel, compared Stephen's ability to that of Mozart, who was able to compose an entire symphony in his head. Physicist Kip Thorne said Stephen had learned to manipulate mental images of shapes not only in three dimensions but in four.

One evening in November 1970, shortly after Lucy's birth, Stephen had a revelation. It happened while he was getting into bed—a very slow process for him. He had been thinking about black holes, those frighteningly powerful regions of space that suck up everything, and from which nothing can escape. Black holes had been on his mind lately because of his work on collapsing stars and singularities. He knew that all black holes have a singularity at their center. Stephen's revelation that evening was that a black hole can never get smaller, and that is because of the event horizon.

⋛ EVENT HORIZON ⋛

The event horizon can best be pictured as a circle surrounding a black hole. Inside the circle, gravity is too strong to allow anything to escape. In order to escape, a particle would need to travel faster than the speed of light, which, as Einstein proved, is impossible. If a star collapses to form a black hole, photons (light particles) emitted by the collapsing star will get stuck at the event horizon. These photons, traveling at the speed of light, are too fast to be dragged into the black hole, but not fast enough to escape, so they remain there, hovering.

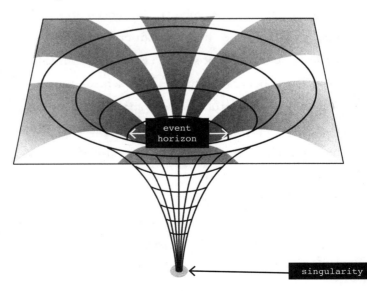

Stephen realized that if these photons collide with each other, it will change their direction, and they will fall back into the black hole, adding to its mass and making it bigger. But they can never escape the black hole. In other words, a black hole can only stay the same size or get bigger. It can never get smaller. Stephen lay in bed all night thinking about his discovery. First thing in the morning, he called his colleague Roger Penrose and told him about it. Roger immediately knew Stephen was onto something.

DO BLACK HOLES HAVE ENTROPY?

Both Stephen and Roger realized that Stephen's new theory of black holes resembled a well-known law of physics called the second law of thermodynamics, which concerns something called entropy. Entropy is the amount of disorder in the universe. The second law states that entropy always increases over time. To give a simple example of this, you can break an egg, but you can never put that egg back together again. In other words, the direction of travel in the universe is always toward more disorder, not more order. Stephen was saying that a black hole is like entropy, because it can only increase over time.

But this raised a puzzling question: What if something disordered (like a broken egg) were to fall into a black hole? It would essentially be lost, so the amount of entropy in the universe would *decrease*, breaking the second law of thermodynamics. A young graduate student named Jacob Bekenstein suggested a way out of this problem. He said that black holes aren't just *like* entropy; they must *have* entropy. If something falls into the black hole, it adds to the hole's entropy, so the second law still holds.

Stephen didn't think much of Bekenstein's idea. He pointed out that if a black hole has entropy, then it must have heat. If something has heat, it must radiate energy, and everyone knew that black holes don't radiate anything, because nothing can escape their gravitational pull. Stephen joined forces with two other physicists, James Bardeen and Brandon Carter, to explore these ideas in more detail. Together, they came up with three more theories of black hole mechanics.

Stephen's work with Bardeen and Carter showed that there are strong similarities between black holes and the laws of thermodynamics. This suggested that Bekenstein might be right after all, and that maybe black holes do have entropy. In 1973, Stephen decided to try a new approach. Perhaps the solution to the problem lay in the field of quantum mechanics—the world of the very small.

> I considered how particles and fields governed by quantum theory would behave near a black hole.

Quantum Mechanics

Quantum mechanics looks at the world of particles—such as atoms, photons, and electrons—and how they behave and interact. At the quantum scale, things can be very bizarre. For example:

→ Light sometimes behaves as a particle (a photon) and sometimes as a wave.

→ The speed and the position of a particle can never be known at the same time. (This is called the uncertainty principle.)

→ Particles can spontaneously pop into existence and then disappear.

HAWKING RADIATION

Stephen knew that on the quantum scale, there is no such thing as completely empty space. Even in a vacuum, particles continually pop in and out of existence. It works like this: A pair of particles will appear, one with positive energy, the other with negative energy. Almost instantly they will collide and destroy each other. This happens all the time in the world around us.

Stephen calculated that on the event horizon of a black hole, pairs of particles will pop into existence as they do everywhere else. But the gravity around a black hole is so powerful that the particle pair won't always destroy each other. Instead, they can separate. The negative particle will cross the event horizon and get sucked into the black hole, but the positive particle won't necessarily follow: it might escape the black hole. In other words, a black hole *can* radiate energy. Bekenstein had been right! Yet it was Stephen who proved it, and in due course, these black hole emissions would become known as Hawking radiation.

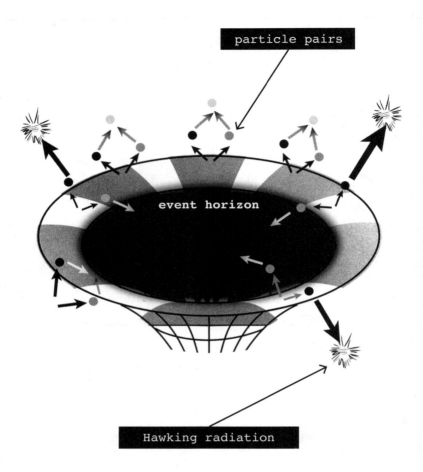

Stephen also realized something else: when a black hole absorbs a negative particle, that particle will carry negative energy into the black hole, reducing its energy. With his equation $E = mc^2$, Einstein showed that energy is mass in another form. In other words, the black hole loses mass. It gets smaller. It may even evaporate eventually, although there probably isn't enough time for that to happen before the universe itself ends. Thus, Stephen was able to prove that his theory about black holes never shrinking doesn't always hold true.

Stephen's discoveries were truly astounding and overturned much of what scientists believed about black holes. Furthermore, by showing how quantum events affect black holes, he had found a way of linking the two great theories of physics: quantum mechanics and Einstein's general relativity. His breakthrough on black holes was an important step on the road toward a "theory of everything."

A Theory of Everything

Quantum mechanics explains how the world works at the scale of the very small, while Einstein's theory of general relativity explains how the world works on the scale of the large. The trouble is, they describe what seem like two different universes. At large scales, gravity is the dominant force; in the quantum world, three other forces—electromagnetism and the strong and weak nuclear forces—hold sway. The great challenge of physics over the past century has been to find a "theory of everything," a set of laws that describes how the universe works at all scales.

⇒ PRESENTING THE DISCOVERY ⇐

Stephen told his colleagues about his discovery in January 1974. It caused huge excitement. His friend Martin Rees told Dennis Sciama: "Have you heard? Stephen's changed everything!" Roger Penrose phoned Stephen, who was just sitting down to his birthday dinner with family and guests. Penrose was so excited, he kept Stephen talking for ages, and the food got cold.

Stephen formally presented his idea at a conference in Oxford in February. It was met with a baffled silence. Many in the audience didn't understand Stephen's arguments. Those who did were shocked. How could anything come out of a black hole? The conference chairman, Professor John Taylor, eventually spoke up.

Undaunted by this reaction, Stephen published his paper on the discovery in the science magazine *Nature*. Very soon, it was the hot topic of discussion for physicists all over the world. Dennis Sciama called Stephen's paper "one of the most beautiful in the history of physics." Top cosmologist John Wheeler, who had popularized the term "black hole," said Stephen's discovery was like "rolling candy on the tongue." That spring, Stephen was elected a fellow of the Royal Society. At thirty-two, he was one of the youngest ever to receive this honor. By 1976, Hawking radiation had been accepted by the vast majority of theoretical physicists.

≥ CALIFORNIA ≤

In 1974, Kip Thorne, a physics professor at the California Institute of Technology (Caltech), invited Stephen and his family to spend a year as his guests in California. He and Stephen had been friends since 1965, and he was eager to work with him on black holes. The Hawkings— along with Stephen's assistant, Bernard Carr—flew out in August. They were offered every comfort—a spacious house, a car, medical expenses, schooling for Robert and Lucy, and an electric wheelchair for Stephen. He was excited by the increased mobility and was soon zooming around in it.

THE BET

In December 1974, Stephen and Kip made a bet. Kip bet Stephen that Cygnus X-1, part of a binary star system—a pair of stars circling each other—about six thousand light-years from Earth, was a black hole. At this time, black holes were still theoretical. No one had yet found one. Being black, they are impossible to see, but they can be detected by their effect on objects around them. This is most observable in the case of a binary star system. If astronomers see a star behaving as if it is in a binary star system, but it appears to be on its own, then the object it is circling might be a black hole. This was the case with Cygnus X-1. Another clue to detecting a black hole is the presence of X-rays, which are generated when a black hole sucks material from its companion star. Cygnus X-1 was a major source of X-rays.

The only doubt that it wasn't a black hole was its mass. If it was under a certain mass (just over twice the mass of our sun), then it could be a neutron star—

a very small, dense, partly collapsed star. Astronomers couldn't be sure what its mass was, hence the bet. Actually, Stephen agreed with Kip that it probably was a black hole, but if it turned out not to be, he thought his disappointment would be eased by winning the bet!

CHAPTER 4

GROWING FAME

During his trip to California, Stephen became so used to buzzing around in an electric wheelchair that the family raided its savings to purchase one for him in Cambridge. On his return there, the university made Stephen a reader (the highest grade of academic below professor) and gave him his own secretary, Judy Fella, who would handle all of Stephen's administration and travel bookings. Also, a new graduate student, Don Page, joined the household. He would go on to become a long-term friend and collaborator with Stephen.

Universities in the UK: Academic Titles

PhD student: A graduate student working to obtain a PhD.

Postdoctoral research fellow: A researcher who has earned a PhD and goes on to further specialize in a particular field.

Lecturer: Similar to an assistant professor in the US, lecturers teach undergraduates and conduct research.

Senior lecturer: Similar to an associate professor in the US, senior lecturers lead research groups and supervise graduate students.

Reader: A senior academic, often with an international reputation, whose role mainly involves research.

Professor: The most senior academic position in the UK. In addition to research and teaching, professors take on leadership roles in their department or faculty.

These changes gave Jane more free time to pursue her interest in music and singing. She joined the choir of St. Mark's Church in Cambridge. There, she became friends with the organist, Jonathan Hellyer Jones. Jonathan became a regular visitor to the Hawking home. He taught eight-year-old Lucy to play the piano and assisted Stephen with his physical needs.

In the autumn of 1977, Stephen was promoted to the position of chair of gravitational physics and became Professor Stephen Hawking. The following February, he went to London on the occasion of Prince Charles's admission to the Royal Society. While he was demonstrating his wheelchair to the fascinated prince, he accidentally ran over Charles's toes!

This wasn't the only time he had run over someone's toes, and there were some who suggested he did it to people who irritated him.

A malicious rumor. I'll run over anyone who repeats it.

Stephen's name was becoming increasingly well known across the academic community, and he was honored with numerous medals and awards, including:

> The Eddington Medal
> The Hughes Medal
> The Albert Einstein Award
> The Dannie Heineman Prize for Mathematical Physics
> The James Clerk Maxwell Medal

In 1979, Stephen was named Lucasian Professor of Mathematics at Cambridge University, a position held by Sir Isaac Newton 310 years earlier. Stephen was given his own private office and managed to scrawl his name in a large book that all new university tutors must sign. It would be the last time he would ever sign his name. His illness was getting steadily worse, and even small movements were increasingly difficult. By the late 1970s, his speech was so slurred, he could only be understood by his family and closest friends. When he gave public talks and lectures, one of his research students would usually act as interpreter.

Despite this, Stephen never lost his zest for life. He especially loved trying out reckless maneuvers in his wheelchair. On a 1981 visit to San Francisco, he suddenly took off down one of the city's steepest streets in his electric wheelchair. When his colleagues finally caught up with him at the bottom, they found him grinning happily and insisting that they take him to an even steeper hill.

THE INFORMATION PARADOX

It was during that trip to San Francisco that Stephen first talked about an issue that had been troubling him since at least 1974. There was a problem, he said, at the heart of his equations for Hawking radiation—a problem that threatened our entire understanding of the laws of physics. Stephen called it the "information paradox." Put simply, if a black hole can shrink and eventually disappear, then what happens to all the information that went into the black hole?

"Information," in this sense, is not only the physical objects that fell in, but everything about those objects, such as their mass and the location where they fell in. This presented a problem for quantum mechanics, which states that information can never be lost. It can be jumbled, warped, twisted, or changed in all sorts of ways, but not lost. For example, if you burn a book, the book and all the information contained within it is transformed into a heap of ashes. But the book isn't completely lost. It could, in theory, and with great difficulty, be reconstructed from those ashes.

This is not the case with black holes. It was already known before Stephen's discovery that information could be lost inside a black hole. However, this wasn't such a problem, because the information, although beyond our reach, still existed in this universe, so it didn't violate the laws of quantum mechanics. But if a black hole could disappear, that suggested the information really was lost—and for physicists that was a problem.

When Stephen first mentioned the information paradox in 1981, it sparked a major debate in physics—a debate that goes on to this day.

Some physicists argued that the information is somehow retained in the form of Hawking radiation (see page 65). Stephen disagreed. Hawking radiation comes from positive particles splitting off from their negative pairs at the event horizon—it doesn't come from inside the black hole itself. If it did, that would violate Einstein's theory of general relativity, which states that nothing can escape from inside the event horizon of a black hole.

Some physicists, such as Leonard Susskind, saw a bigger problem in the information paradox. If information could be lost, that would threaten the whole principle of cause and effect, which was fundamental to physics. Scientists had always believed that an unbreakable chain of cause and effect links the past, present, and future, from the big bang to the end of the universe. The information paradox suggested that this chain could be broken.

"Stephen had a 'Stephen' look on his face, a little smile that says, 'You may not believe it but I'm right, no mistake about it.' We were absolutely sure Stephen was wrong but we couldn't see why."
—Leonard Susskind, recalling the moment Stephen revealed the information paradox

Laplace's Demon

To understand the threat the information paradox posed to cause-and-effect, we need to look at the work of French mathematician Pierre-Simon Laplace (1749—1827). Laplace asked us to imagine a supernatural "demon" that knows the precise location and momentum of every particle in the universe at any moment in time. Because every particle's movement has a cause and an effect, it should be possible, with that knowledge, for the demon to calculate the entire history and future of the universe. But if information could be lost inside an evaporating black hole, it would mean that Laplace was wrong, and the past and future are not fixed or knowable but random.

Thanks to Stephen Hawking, I can no longer be certain of anything!

⋛ INFLATION THEORY ⋚

In the early 1980s, Stephen became involved in a debate about the very early history of the universe. A physicist named Alan Guth had come up with a theory called inflation, which seemed to solve one of the biggest problems of the big bang theory. The problem was that evidence from CMBR (see page 44) suggested that the early universe was smooth—it had the same texture throughout, without any lumpiness. Yet today's universe is "lumpy," with clusters of galaxies and stars alongside vast reaches of empty space. No one could understand how one could produce the other.

Then Guth suggested that just after the big bang, the universe underwent a very brief phase of rapid expansion, or inflation. His equations showed that this could have led to the lumpy universe we know today. Inflation theory was very promising, but it had problems, and Stephen came up with a modification to make it work better. Another important contributor to the debate was Russian physicist Andrei Linde, who had proposed his own improvements to inflation theory.

In 1981, Stephen went to a debate in Moscow, where he gave a talk on the subject. Andrei volunteered to translate for the Russian-speaking audience. All went well at first. Andrei was delighted to hear Stephen say that he, Andrei Linde, had recently suggested an interesting solution to the problems of inflation theory. But then Stephen proceeded to tell everyone what was wrong with Andrei's solution!

Linde was forced to spend a very painful half hour translating Stephen's criticism of his own work. At the conclusion of the talk, Andrei told the audience that he had faithfully translated Stephen's words, but he didn't agree with them, and he explained why. He then invited Stephen to continue the debate in private, which they did. They talked for over two hours.

A UNIVERSE WITH NO BOUNDARIES

Stephen's research into the very early universe led him to some startling conclusions. In 1983, he published a paper with American physicist James Hartle describing what they termed the "no-boundary proposal." In this, they suggested that there might be no boundary—that is, no beginning or ending—to the universe. This was not to say that Stephen had lost faith in the big bang theory. What he was arguing was that scientists' whole understanding of the big bang was mistaken. In their paper, Hawking and Hartle asked readers to imagine traveling backward in time toward the very beginning of the universe.

THIS WAY TO **THE BIG BANG!**

As we approach the singularity that gave rise to the big bang, they wrote, everything becomes extremely compressed. It becomes so compressed that the differences between space and time disappear. Time becomes like another dimension of space. This is, of course, impossible for us to imagine with our human brains. Time isn't normally something we can see or touch—it's just the flow of events.

But what happens in the extremely early universe is that space and time merge to form something called four-dimensional space. (You can't picture this, so don't even try!) This four-dimensional space curves around to become a closed surface, like a ball. A ball is not infinite in size, yet it has no edge or boundary, so anyone traveling across the ball's surface might think it is infinite.

And this, according to Hawking and Hartle, is how we should try to imagine the universe: not infinite, yet with no boundaries—no beginning or ending.

This idea boggles our minds because we're so used to thinking that everything that exists must have started at some point. We're tempted to ask the question: "What happened before the big bang?" But when time has become part of space, to ask what happened before it makes no sense. As Stephen says, it's like asking what's south of the South Pole.

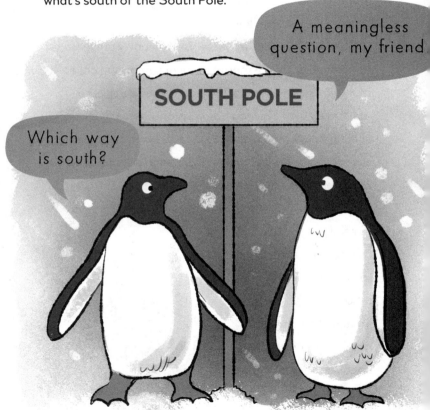

CHAPTER 5

A BRIEF HISTORY OF TIME

In 1982, Stephen decided to write a popular book about cosmology, a book that would reach beyond his usual readership of scientists and appeal to ordinary readers. He would explain in simple terms what was known about the universe, how it began, and how it might end. He had a practical reason for writing the book: he needed to make some money to pay for his daughter's schooling. However, he also saw it as an opportunity to share some of the exciting new discoveries in cosmology with the wider public.

⇒ CHOOSING A PUBLISHER ⇐

Stephen contacted a literary agent—a person who deals with publishers on behalf of an author—and said he wanted to write a science book about the origin, development, and eventual fate of the universe that would sell in airport bookstores. The agent agreed to take Stephen on but advised him to lower his expectations. Such a book might sell well to students and academics but would never be a bestseller. Stephen disagreed.

By 1984, he had finished the first draft of the book. He approached Cambridge University Press, which had published his other books. The publisher suggested the book might sell about twenty thousand copies a year worldwide. Stephen thought he could do better than that. His agent sent the book out to various publishers. Several turned it down, but a few made offers. Against his agent's advice, Stephen decided to sign with Bantam, a mass-market publisher that had little experience with science books, but whose books did tend to sell well in airports.

⋛ LIFE-OR-DEATH DECISION ⋚

After receiving suggestions from his editor at Bantam, Stephen went to work on a second draft of the book. In the summer of 1985, he traveled to Geneva, Switzerland, where he rented an apartment. He planned to revise the book there and do some scientific research at the European Organization for Nuclear Research (CERN), which was based nearby.

CERN

CERN is a major center of research into particle physics, the study of subatomic particles. Here, physicists use particle accelerators to discover what the universe is made of at the most fundamental level, and how it works. A particle accelerator is a machine that speeds up particles to extremely high rates and collides them with other particles. By observing the effects of these collisions, physicists can learn about the structure of the subatomic world and the laws governing it.

Shortly after arriving in Geneva, Stephen came down with pneumonia and was rushed to the hospital. His lungs, already weakened by his illness, were struggling to cope. He was having choking fits and finding it hard to breathe. In a bid to save his life, the doctors placed him in a temporary coma and put him on a ventilator, a machine that helps a patient breathe. By a remarkable coincidence, one of the doctors at the hospital had earlier that evening watched a TV program about Stephen and knew he had ALS. He was therefore aware of what drugs he could and couldn't give to his patient.

When Jane found out what had happened, she rushed to Geneva. The doctors told her the only way to save Stephen's life was to perform a tracheotomy. This involved making a cut in the front of his neck and inserting a hollow tube into his windpipe, so he could breathe without the use of his nose or mouth. Unfortunately, this meant he would lose what remained of his voice.

It was a terrible decision for Jane to have to make. Without his voice, and with his body virtually immobile, how would Stephen be able to communicate? She feared it would mean the end of his career and any meaningful sort of life. Would he even want to continue living in such a condition? But Jane didn't hesitate. She knew that Stephen would want to live, no matter what obstacles he might face. She told the doctors to perform the operation.

> "It was my decision . . . but I have sometimes thought—what have I done? What sort of life have I let him in for?"
> —Jane Hawking

A NEW VOICE

When he was strong enough to travel, Stephen was flown back to Britain, and the operation was carried out at Addenbrooke's Hospital in Cambridge. For the remainder of his life, he would breathe through a small opening in his throat around the height of his shirt collar.

Three months after his operation, Stephen was able to return home, but his life would never be the same. From then on, he would need round-the-clock nursing care. The only way he could communicate was by spelling out words letter by letter, raising his eyebrow when someone pointed to the correct letter on an alphabet card.

In 1986, a computer programmer from California named Walt Woltosz offered Stephen a much more efficient means of communicating. Woltosz had created a computer program called the Equalizer, which enabled Stephen to move a handheld clicker to select words, phrases, or single letters from a computer screen. Once he had prepared something to say, the computer would turn it into speech. Using the Equalizer, Stephen was able to produce up to fifteen words a minute.

It was a bit slow, but then I think slowly, so it suited me well.

The Equalizer may have been slow, but at least Stephen could now speak with a voice that everyone could understand, and he no longer depended on an interpreter. After Stephen achieved worldwide fame through his book, people would listen to him give speeches with this strange, computerized voice, and it became a big part of his identity. So much so that later on, when new technology opened up the possibility of a different, more natural-sounding voice, he decided not to change it.

⋛ BIRTH OF A BESTSELLER ⋛

Soon Stephen was strong enough to go back to work on his book. His editor at Bantam, Peter Guzzardi, was not a scientist, and he struggled to understand some of the book's ideas. He figured that what he couldn't understand, the general public wouldn't, either, so he sent it back to Stephen, asking him to simplify the more complicated passages. Stephen would rewrite them and return the text to Peter. The editor would then often come back with further requests for explanations. This would happen time after time, and Stephen began to get irritated. But in the end, he came around to Peter's point of view.

> "My primary contribution to the book was to doggedly keep asking Stephen questions, not giving up until I understood what he intended to convey."
> —Peter Guzzardi

> "At times I thought the process would never end. But [Peter] was right: it is a much better book as a result."
> —Stephen Hawking

Peter and Stephen agreed on one thing: the book should not contain equations. Cambridge University Press had warned Stephen that every equation he included would cut book sales in half. In the end, he limited himself to just one equation—the most famous one of all: Einstein's $E = mc^2$.

Another important contribution that Peter made was to the title: Stephen wanted to call the book *From the Big Bang to Black Holes: A Short History of Time*. Peter changed this to the snappier *A Brief History of Time*. Stephen later called the title "a stroke of genius."

A Brief History of Time came out in the United States in April 1988 and in the UK in June of that year. From the moment of its launch, the book proved astoundingly popular. The first printing sold out in a matter of days, and the publishers struggled to print enough to meet demand. After rapidly rising to the top of the bestseller charts in both countries, the book remained there week after week. It was soon a worldwide hit, after being translated into dozens of different languages. Today, more than ten million copies have been sold—quite a few of them at airport bookstores.

> "If we find the answer to [the theory of everything], it would be the ultimate triumph of human reason—for then we should know the mind of God."
> —the famous final sentence from *A Brief History of Time*

It's hard to explain how a book about cosmology and quantum mechanics could be so popular. A large part of it must have had to do with the quality of the writing. Stephen's use of analogy—comparisons with everyday things we can relate to—helped make complex scientific ideas more accessible, and his sense of humor won over many readers. Editor Peter Guzzardi also played an important role in making the book simple enough to be understood by the average reader.

Even so, there were many who admitted they didn't understand it. Some critics mischievously suggested that most people bought it not to read but to display on their bookshelves to show how clever they were. Stephen was annoyed by this comment and hit back: "They feel that they, the critics, are very clever people, and if they can't understand my book completely, then ordinary mortals have no chance."

> "Each day I get a pile of letters about that book, many asking questions or making detailed comments that indicate that they have read it, even if they don't understand all of it. I also get stopped by strangers on the street who tell me how much they enjoyed it."
> —Stephen Hawking

CELEBRITY SCIENTIST

Another factor in the book's success was undoubtedly Stephen himself. People were fascinated by the story of a scientific genius who had managed to overcome his disability to achieve so much. He became an iconic and instantly recognizable figure. Admirers in Chicago even started a Stephen Hawking fan club.

Stephen traveled a great deal to promote the book. He was profiled in magazines around the world and was the subject of several television documentaries. Universities showered him with honorary degrees, and he received several major international awards. These included the Wolf Prize in Physics, an annual prize awarded by the Wolf Foundation in Israel, which he won jointly with Roger Penrose in 1988. All this publicity left him with little time for his students. Some of his colleagues grew resentful of the book's success and the attention it brought to its author, believing it had more to do with his difficult circumstances than his work itself.

Stephen often surprised his hosts with his energy during foreign trips. On one visit to New York to publicize his book, he noticed there was a dance going on in the ballroom of the hotel where he was staying.

His hosts, all distinguished physicists, were ready for bed, but Stephen insisted they crash the dance. So they followed him in and could only watch in awe as he joyfully twirled around the dance floor in his wheelchair.

MARRIAGE BREAKUP

For many years now, Jane and Stephen's life together had been very difficult. In public, they continued to project the image of a happily married couple, but both of them were under enormous strain and turned to other people for support. Since Stephen's operation in 1985, the constant presence of nurses in the household meant less privacy for everyone, and there was little chance of an ordinary family life. Stephen had always been very focused on his work and now traveled a lot to publicize his book. Stephen and Jane had different ideas about religion, too.

Jane and Jonathan Hellyer Jones had become close, while Stephen and one of his nurses, Elaine Mason, spent increasing amounts of time together. In 1990, Stephen and Jane agreed to separate, although they still lived near each other in Cambridge. Five years later, they divorced, having been married for thirty years. In 1995, Stephen married Elaine; two years later, Jane married Jonathan.

SETTLING THE BET

In the years that followed Stephen's bet with Kip Thorne that Cygnus X-1 was not a black hole (see page 71), evidence had emerged that made it 95 percent certain that it was one. In June 1990, sixteen years after the bet, Stephen was visiting Caltech, Kip's university, when he decided it was time to settle it. Kip was away in Moscow at the time, so Stephen, with the help of some friends, broke into his office, where the framed bet hung on the wall, and wrote a note conceding that he had been wrong. He signed it with his thumbprint.

WORMHOLES AND BABY UNIVERSES

Despite the demands of fame, Stephen found time to continue working on his scientific theories. In the late 1980s, he developed a new theory about how the universe could work at very small scales. He proposed that at the quantum level, where even empty space becomes chaotic, with particles constantly appearing and disappearing (see page 64), it was possible that tiny black holes known as wormholes could flicker briefly into existence. On the far end of these wormholes, miniature universes could form.

This, he suggested, could be happening all the time, within us and around us. Usually these baby universes would disappear along with the wormhole. But occasionally, one might expand into a separate universe with its own galaxies, stars, and planets. He speculated that this might have been how our own universe began. Perhaps ours was just one of countless universes linked by wormholes in an infinite lattice.

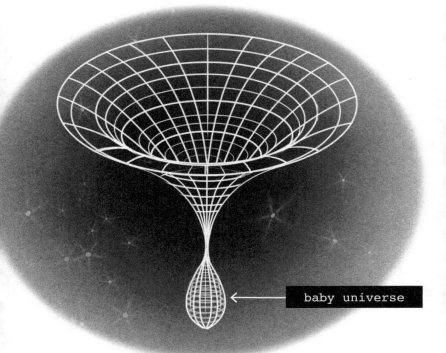

baby universe

Stephen believed that this theory might help explain a mystery that had puzzled physicists for a long time: Why are things like the masses of particles and the laws of nature as they are? The numbers of the universe seem random. Yet if they were even slightly different—if gravity were slightly stronger or weaker, for example—life wouldn't be possible, and we wouldn't exist. Perhaps they are as they are because this is just one of many universes—one that happened to be capable of producing life.

TIME TRAVEL

In the 1980s, physicists discussed the possibility of wormholes connecting not only to other universes but also to different places and times in our own universe. Kip Thorne suggested it might be possible for an advanced civilization to develop a method of holding open the throat of a wormhole to allow someone to transport themselves backward in time. Stephen didn't think this was possible, partly because of the "grandfather paradox."

The Grandfather Paradox

The grandfather paradox is often used to explain why time travel to the past must be impossible. If you went back in time and killed your grandfather as a child, it would mean that you were never born. But if you were never born, you wouldn't be able to go back in time to kill your grandfather. However, if your grandfather was alive, you would be born, so you *could* go back in time to kill your grandfather—and so on.

In 1992, Stephen proposed something called the "chronology protection conjecture." Put simply, this states that the time-machine wormhole would explode if anyone tried to use it. As Stephen explained, this would "keep the universe safe for historians"—and grandfathers!

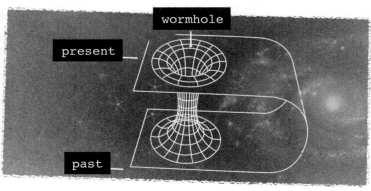

MOVIE OF THE BOOK

In 1989, work began on a movie version of *A Brief History of Time*. It was to be produced by Steven Spielberg and directed by Errol Morris. Stephen Hawking hoped the movie would use spectacular visual effects to bring to life the scientific concepts he had explained in his book. However, Spielberg insisted that a big part of the film had to be about Stephen himself; otherwise people wouldn't pay to see it, he said. Stephen reluctantly accepted this and agreed to narrate it. He also worked closely with Morris on the editing process. The movie *A Brief History of Time* premiered in 1991. It won numerous awards, and most critics gave it high marks.

> "An elegant, inspirational and mysterious movie"
> —David Ansen in *Newsweek*

CHAPTER 6

NEW THEORIES

Despite occasional health scares, Stephen's condition was fairly stable during the 1990s. He kept up a hectic program of international travel, even finding time to visit Antarctica in 1997. (He didn't get as far as the South Pole, so he was unable to personally verify that there's nothing to the south of it.) He was portrayed in the TV shows *The Simpsons* and *Dilbert*, and his son Tim introduced Stephen to Formula 1 racing and rock concerts. Stephen, who loved classical music, left one of these concerts after just twenty minutes.

There should be no boundaries to human endeavor. We are all different.

The Simpsons

In 1999, an animated version of Stephen appeared in the popular TV series *The Simpsons*. In the course of the episode, Stephen's fictionalized wheelchair is shown to contain an extraordinary array of devices, which he uses to brush his teeth, punch his enemies with a boxing glove, and even fly. At the end, Stephen says to Homer Simpson: "Your theory of a doughnut-shaped universe is intriguing, Homer. I may have to steal it."

THE NAKED SINGULARITY

Back in 1970, Roger Penrose had proposed that in a black hole, a singularity must always be "clothed" by an event horizon. In the decades that followed, this provoked a great deal of debate among physicists. In 1991, Stephen bet Kip Thorne and John Preskill, another physicist at Caltech, that Penrose was right, and there was no such thing as a "naked singularity." But during the 1990s, the physicist Demetrios Christodoulou made calculations showing that under very unusual conditions, such as a collapsing black hole, a singularity might occur without an event horizon. It would be about as likely as a pencil balancing on its tip, but not impossible. In 1997, Stephen publicly conceded the bet, and appropriately, he presented the winners with some clothing: a pair of T-shirts.

GIVE PEAS A CHANCE

In 1998, it was discovered that the universe wasn't just expanding—its expansion was actually speeding up. This was a big moment in cosmology, and it gave rise to new theories about a mysterious force known as dark energy.

It also seemed to be bad news for Stephen Hawking and Jim Hartle's theory about a no-boundary universe (see page 84). Their theory predicted that the universe would eventually stop expanding and start to shrink, ultimately collapsing in a so-called "big crunch." The new discovery appeared to contradict this, suggesting instead that the universe would keep on expanding forever. So Stephen, together with South African physicist Neil Turok, began to look at the problem again to see if they could save the no-boundary model.

The result of their discussions was a new theory that time and space began with something they called an instanton. This was an exceedingly tiny, wrinkled, four-dimensional sphere that existed for a very brief instant before inflating itself into an infinite, ever-expanding universe. The instanton contained matter, gravity, space, and time in compressed form. It was not like the singularity in the original no-boundary model, because it was not infinitely dense and small. Yet it was similar to it, because nothing existed outside or before it.

Stephen and Neil calculated that the instanton would have had the mass and shape of a wrinkled pea, though it was much, much smaller than that. This was, perhaps, an unfortunate comparison to make, because the media immediately started calling it a "pea" rather than an instanton. Nevertheless, the introduction of the instanton appeared to save the no-boundary model, because it allowed for an ever-expanding universe.

Soon, however, the idea began attracting criticism from other physicists. Some pointed out that many of the universes the instanton might produce would have no matter in them. Andrei Linde calculated that the universes produced by the instanton would have, at best, only about one-thirtieth of the matter of our universe.

> "A number of times [Stephen] has come up with surprising conclusions that at first seem like they are wrong. But in several instances, he turned out to be right. In other cases, he was wrong. We will just have to wait and see which it is this time."
> —Andrei Linde, commenting on Stephen's instanton theory

Stephen and Neil responded by saying that their simple model needed some tinkering but that the basic principle was sound. The debate became heated, and popular science magazines eagerly reported on the dispute. One headline in *Astronomy* magazine read:

GIVE PEAS A CHANCE

BIRTHDAY PARTY

In January 2002, Stephen turned sixty, and his friends planned a big party. However, just a few days before the event, he suffered a serious accident. While traveling along uneven pavement near his home, he lost control of his wheelchair and crashed into a wall. The wheelchair overturned, and he broke his hip.

Because of his frail condition, the doctors could only give him a local anesthetic, so he was conscious as they performed emergency surgery on him. In typical fashion, Stephen made light of the incident: "I had an argument with a wall ... and the wall won." He insisted that the party proceed as planned, and so it did, attended by about two hundred guests, including family, friends, colleagues, and former students. Elaine had a special birthday present planned: a flight in a hot-air balloon.

Stephen's friends all had something to say on his birthday:

"I am very glad to note that Stephen has now . . . officially become an old man, so that he can . . . get away with saying . . . outrageous things. Of course Stephen has always done that kind of thing."
—Roger Penrose

"I've often suspected there must be more than one Stephen Hawking to have made so many important discoveries. I would like to wish all of them a very happy sixtieth birthday!"
—Bernard Carr

"Stephen, as we all know, is by far the most stubborn and infuriating person in the universe."
—Leonard Susskind

By 2003, Stephen was finding it increasingly difficult to activate the Equalizer's handheld clicker device. As a result, his ability to communicate slowed down. This must have been immensely frustrating for him, because his mind remained as quick as ever and was brimming with ideas. To try to speed things up, he employed a graduate student, Christophe Galfard, to listen to his theories and test them mathematically to see if they worked. Christophe found it tough waiting for Stephen to express his thoughts, so he began completing Stephen's sentences for him. When others had tried this in the past, Stephen had ignored them and gone on forming the sentence as if they hadn't spoken. This time, however, Stephen allowed it. Christophe also sped up communication by watching for the tiny movements in Stephen's face that indicated "yes" or "no," rather than waiting for him to select the word on the screen.

> "I've never really had a problem communicating with [Stephen]. I know we understand each other very well; there's eye contact. . . . You know, because I can suggest an idea, and he will say, 'No, that's wrong.' And then I will . . . [say], 'Is it wrong for this reason?'"
> —Christophe Galfard

ANOTHER BET

The debate about the information paradox, which Stephen first introduced in 1981 (see page 77), continued to divide physicists. Stephen still believed that information was lost inside a black hole, and even made another of his famous bets about it.

He and Kip Thorne bet John Preskill that since general relativity states that nothing can escape from a black hole, Hawking radiation must emit "new" information. In other words, the laws of quantum mechanics must be rewritten. Preskill argued the opposite, that information emitted by Hawking radiation is related in some way to the information that had fallen into the black hole, and it is general relativity that needs amending.

In 2003, Leonard Susskind and another physicist, Juan Martín Maldacena, produced a new theory offering a solution to the information paradox. They suggested that at the event horizon of a black hole, reality actually splits in two. From the perspective of someone outside the black hole—let's call her Jill—watching her friend Jack falling toward it, Jack becomes trapped at the event horizon. Jill sees him flatten out and heat up, and then later get emitted as Hawking radiation.

But from Jack's perspective, he will cross over the event horizon as if it weren't there, and fall into the singularity. In other words, information is both lost and not lost from our universe, depending on the viewpoint. That way, the paradox is resolved and the laws of quantum mechanics and general relativity are not broken.

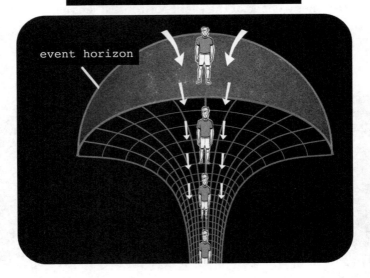

Stephen was not convinced by this theory, but it got him thinking once again about the information paradox. Unfortunately, his work was interrupted in December 2003, when he fell seriously ill with pneumonia again. He was rushed to the hospital and placed on life support.

His family and friends readied themselves for his death, but Stephen was sure his time was not up yet. He spent the weeks in the hospital thinking about the information paradox, determined to find a new approach. In March 2004, he was strong enough to return home, and he and Christophe set to work on the ideas he had come up with, rejecting some and honing others, trying to find a way through the problem. By July, he was ready to unveil his conclusions, which he planned to do at a conference in Dublin, Ireland.

> "I have solved the black hole information problem and I want to talk about it."
> —Stephen Hawking to the chair of the Dublin conference

⋛ A SOLUTION ⋚

Stephen's request to speak came late, once the conference program had already been organized. If anyone but Stephen Hawking had asked, the organizers probably would have said no.

Speaking to an audience of more than six hundred

physicists and dozens of journalists in Dublin, Stephen said he was ready to concede the bet that he and Kip had made with John Preskill: information was *not* lost inside a black hole. However, Stephen did not believe that Susskind and Maldacena's solution was correct. Nor did he believe, as he once had, that information could disappear down a wormhole into another universe. Instead, he proposed a new solution: that the event horizon allows information to escape in a garbled form.

> "I'm sorry to disappoint science fiction fans, but... there is no possibility of using black holes to travel to other universes. If you jump into a black hole, your mass energy will be returned to our universe, but in a mangled form which contains the information about what you were like."
> —Stephen Hawking, Dublin, July 2004

Most of the physicists in the audience were baffled by Stephen's solution. As for John Preskill, he was delighted to have won the bet but added, "I'll be honest, I didn't understand the talk." Kip Thorne was more polite: "This looks to me on the face of it to be a lovely argument, but I haven't yet seen all the details." Roger Penrose was frustrated with Stephen. "In my view, he was completely wrong to retract [concede the bet]. He should have stuck to his guns."

The terms of the bet stated that the loser should reward the winner with an encyclopedia of the winner's choice. "John is all-American, so naturally he wants an encyclopedia of baseball," said Stephen at the conclusion of his talk. "If Kip agrees to concede the bet later, he can pay me back." The baseball encyclopedia was then brought onstage and handed to Preskill, who proudly held it up over his head like the winner of a sports trophy.

> "The paradox has been argued for thirty years without much progress until I found what I think was its resolution. Information is not lost, but it is not returned in a useful way. It is like burning an encyclopedia. . . . I gave John Preskill a baseball encyclopedia. Maybe I should have just given him the ashes."
> —Stephen Hawking, speaking in January 2005

POPULAR SCIENCE

Throughout the first decade of the twenty-first century, Stephen continued to write books for the general reader. In 2001, he published *The Universe in a Nutshell*. This was, in some senses, a sequel to *A Brief History of Time*, describing the latest developments in physics and cosmology, including such concepts as string theory, M-theory, imaginary time, and extra dimensions. In 2005, he wrote *A Briefer History of Time* with Leonard Mlodinow. This was an update of *A Brief History of Time*, rewritten to make it even more accessible to the general reader.

CHAPTER 7

NOT SLOWING DOWN

By 2005, Stephen's hands had become too weak to use the clicker device he'd relied on for communication, so it was replaced by a new device attached to his glasses. By tensing a cheek muscle, he could activate a sensor to type characters on his keyboard. This was a laborious process, and his communication speed slowed to about a word a minute. But his speed was improved by the addition of some advanced word-predictor software. The software analyzed Stephen's earlier writings, as well as the subject matter of the lecture or paper he was working on, to make accurate predictions about what he was typing.

In the summer of 2006, Stephen and Elaine divorced. Stephen didn't make any public comment at the time. In his only autobiography, *My Brief History*, published in 2013, he refers to various health scares he suffered over the past two decades, during which Elaine was a great support. He writes, "All these crises took their emotional toll on Elaine." For the rest of his life, Stephen would live alone with a housekeeper and his nurses. Following the divorce, he once again became close to Jane and their children and grandchildren.

THE HISTORY OF THE UNIVERSE . . . BACKWARD

In February 2006, Stephen, together with Belgian cosmologist Thomas Hertog, published a paper proposing a remarkable new theory about the universe. One of the big questions that had occupied Stephen for much of his career was "How did the universe begin?" Stephen and Thomas decided to turn this question upside down. Their radical suggestion was that the universe had no single beginning. Instead, they argued, it began in every way imaginable!

In their paper, they asked readers to picture the early universe as fuzzy and indistinct—a collection of every possible early universe, with each one producing a different future. In other words, the past, like the future, is indefinite. As Stephen said in a lecture that year, "There will be a history in which the moon is made of blue cheese, but the [probability] of that is low, which is bad news for mice."

With the past and future uncertain, the only thing that is certain is the present. So instead of trying to determine the history of the universe from its origins to the present day, Stephen and Thomas suggested that people look at the universe as it is now and then work backward to the beginning. That way, we can figure out which of the many possible beginnings is the one most likely to have resulted in the universe we are living in. They called this approach "top-down cosmology."

Stephen discussed the idea further in the 2010 book *The Grand Design*, which he co-wrote with Leonard Mlodinow. Stephen suggested that we throw out the whole concept of cause and effect—the notion that one event leads to another, starting with the big bang onward. Instead, he said, we have to imagine that the present determines which of the infinite number of possible pasts is the correct one. In other words, we create the history of the universe simply by observing it.

> Although we are puny and insignificant on the scale of the cosmos, this makes us in a sense the lords of creation.

Taking this approach, we no longer need to ask ourselves the question that has bothered physicists for decades: Why is the universe fine-tuned for our existence so that everything is perfect for human life? The answer, as Stephen describes it in *The Grand Design*, is that our existence "chooses" the universe we live in, so it was we who fine-tuned it.

Is there any way of testing this idea? In their paper, Stephen and Thomas Hertog suggested we can do it by searching for patterns in the CMBR (see page 44), which is like an echo of the big bang. Super-sensitive detectors on satellites should one day be able to pick up minute variations in the intensity of CMBR to show whether top-down cosmology is indeed correct.

≡ THE GEORGE BOOKS ≡

In 2006, Stephen and his daughter, Lucy, announced they were going to co-author a series of children's books about science and the universe. The first book, *George's Secret Key to the Universe,* was published in 2007. It features a boy, George, and his friends: a scientist named Eric, and Cosmos, the world's most powerful computer. Together, they go on adventures and learn about atoms, stars, planets, moons, and black holes. The Eric character was based on Stephen as he had been before his disability. George's grandmother strongly resembles Stephen's mother, Isobel. The book was popular, and several sequels followed.

> "He has the amazing ability to hold enormous amounts of information in his head, but also to pick out relevant details and make brief comments, which can completely transform your way of thinking."
> —Lucy Hawking on working with her father on the George books

DREAMING OF SPACE

Stephen often talked about the importance of space exploration. He believed that if the human species was to have a long-term future, it would need to one day colonize another planet—not one in our solar system, but an Earth-like planet orbiting another star. In late 2006, Stephen mentioned in an interview that he would love to go into space himself one day. Shortly afterward, Richard Branson, chairman of Virgin Galactic, got in touch with him. Virgin Galactic is a company that plans to take tourists into space. Stephen was offered a place on its debut flight.

The following April, Stephen took his first step toward his goal by taking a flight on a reduced-gravity aircraft. He experienced a total of four minutes of weightlessness during the two-hour flight. It was wonderful for Stephen, who was able to float freely outside his wheelchair and for a brief time felt unconstrained by his paralyzed state. In the end, this was as close as Stephen would ever get to achieving his dream. Sadly, he died before the era of commercial spaceflight.

> "It was amazing. . . . I could have gone on and on. Space, here I come!"
> —Stephen Hawking after his reduced-gravity flight

Reduced-Gravity Aircraft

These craft do not enter space but fly in a certain pattern—climbing steeply, flattening out, and then diving steeply—within the atmosphere. By following this flight path, this type of aircraft offers its passengers around 25 seconds of weightlessness. It begins during the ascent and ends as the aircraft starts to pull out of the dive. The maneuver is repeated numerous times during the flight.

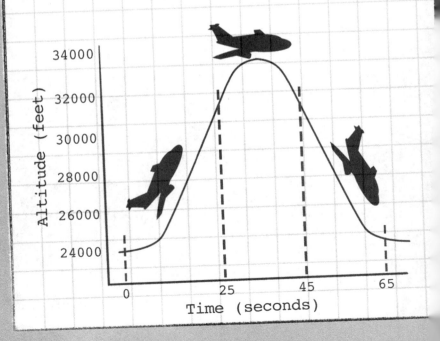

⋝ TIME TRAVELERS PARTY ⋜

On June 28, 2009, Stephen threw a rather unusual party. The invitations were sent out only after the party was over. They read:

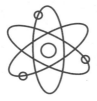

**You are cordially invited
to a reception for time travelers
hosted by Professor Stephen Hawking.**

**To be held in the past,
at the University of Cambridge,
Gonville & Caius College,
Trinity Street, Cambridge.**

The invitations gave the party's date and added: "No RSVP required."

This was a lighthearted test of his proposal in 1992 that time travel to the past is impossible (see page 104). If people had shown up, it would have proved him wrong.

"RETIREMENT"

In September 2009, Stephen retired from his post as Lucasian Professor of Mathematics at Cambridge after thirty years in the role. This followed an age-old custom that Lucasian professors retire at sixty-seven. Stephen wasn't thinking about really retiring, because he was still fizzing with energy and ideas. For the rest of his life, he would continue to work and travel, lecturing about topics such as the colonization of other planets, the origin of life, black holes, and the theory of everything. The only big setback was that he was unable to operate his wheelchair independently after 2009, so he was forced to rely on others to push him.

HAWKING VERSUS HIGGS

In 1964, British physicist Peter Higgs predicted the existence of a particle, later called the Higgs boson, that was necessary to make sense of the generally accepted theory about how the universe works at the quantum scale. Essentially, the Higgs boson was needed to give other particles their mass. The trouble was, the particle was elusive, and perhaps even impossible to observe. In 1996, Stephen predicted that the Higgs boson would never be found. He and Peter Higgs publicly clashed on the issue at a dinner in Edinburgh in 2002.

In 2008, an opportunity finally arrived to observe the Higgs boson, with the opening of the Large Hadron Collider (LHC), a very powerful new particle accelerator at CERN (see page 89).

Stephen commented at the time, "It will be much more exciting if we don't find the Higgs," meaning that quantum theory would have to be rewritten. He added, "Whatever the LHC finds or fails to find, the results will tell us a lot about the structure of the universe."

In January 2012, the month Stephen turned seventy, reports emerged from the LHC that scientists had found the Higgs boson. By June of that year, it had become a near certainty, and the official announcement of the discovery was made on July 4. Stephen was quick to admit he had been wrong, and he suggested that Peter Higgs should win the Nobel Prize, which he later did. At the opening of the Paralympic Games in London the following month, Stephen called the discovery of the Higgs boson "a triumph of human endeavor and international collaboration."

Physics Prize

In March 2013, Stephen was awarded the Breakthrough Prize in Fundamental Physics for his discovery of Hawking radiation. This is a major international award, of similar status to the Nobel Prize. The difference is that the Nobel requires discoveries to have been verified by experiment. At that time, there had been no experimental evidence of Hawking radiation. The award came with a cash prize of $3 million—a welcome boost to Stephen's finances at a time when he was facing increasing costs in nursing care and technological assistance.

THE THEORY OF EVERYTHING

In 2013, filming began on a major motion picture based on Jane Hawking's 2007 memoir about her life with Stephen, *Traveling to Infinity*. The film, titled *The Theory of Everything*, would star Eddie Redmayne as Stephen and Felicity Jones as Jane. Stephen and Jane had read the script ahead of shooting and had given the producers their approval.

One of the first scenes to be filmed for *The Theory of Everything* was the 1963 May Ball at Cambridge University, from early in Stephen and Jane's relationship (see page 50). Stephen visited the set that evening and made quite an impression. Eddie Redmayne described his arrival: "It was dark and beautiful, and then Stephen arrived, silhouetted in his chair. He was spotlighted by his screen [on his wheelchair computer], and on cue, the fireworks went off. It was the greatest entrance I have ever seen in my life."

The film opened in 2014. Stephen had been offered a private screening beforehand. The producers had to wait for about ten minutes in nervous silence as Stephen typed his reaction. In the end, his judgment was positive, if terse: he described it as "broadly true." Later, he called it "a surprisingly honest portrait" of his marriage to Jane. Of Eddie's performance, he said, "At times, I thought it was me."

PLUTO PARTY

In July 2015, the *New Horizons* spacecraft flew past the dwarf planet Pluto, and Stephen celebrated the achievement by throwing a Pluto party. Guests were told to dress up as their favorite celestial object. Stephen dressed as Pluto, Roman god of the underworld. His daughter, Lucy, described the evening: "When darkness fell, we all trooped out into the street to watch a firework display. There, my father [gave a] speech from the pavement on the importance of exploring the solar system. Passers-by must have been surprised at being [lectured] by a man wearing a false white beard, accompanied by a three-headed papier-mâché dog. But this being Cambridge . . . no one called the police."

SOFT HAIR ON BLACK HOLES

To the very end of his life, Stephen never stopped thinking and writing about cosmology. In 2016, just two years before his death, he was part of a team that recommended a startling new approach to solving the black hole information paradox.

Together with physicists Andrew Strominger and Malcolm Perry, Stephen co-wrote a paper titled "Soft Hair on Black Holes." They showed how particles, when entering a black hole, leave a "soft" version of themselves at the event horizon. A soft particle is a particle with energy but no mass. These soft particles, known as super-translations, remain at the event horizon, but they contain information about the particles that have gone into the black hole.

> "The idea is, the super-translations are a hologram of the ingoing particles. Thus they contain all the information that would otherwise be lost."
> —Stephen Hawking

Would it ever be possible to test out this theory? Strominger has worked out that if you add a soft particle to a black hole, it changes the nature of the black hole. Thus, no two black holes are the same—they differ because of the soft particles trapped at their event horizons. In the article, the team suggests that it may be possible, in the future, to detect these differences by analyzing gravitational waves.

Gravitational Waves

Gravitational waves are ripples in space-time caused by some of the most violent events in the universe, such as collapsing stars or colliding black holes. Albert Einstein predicted their existence in 1916 as part of his theory of general relativity. They were first detected on September 14, 2015: a specially built observatory called the Laser Interferometer Gravitational-Wave Observatory (LIGO) sensed gravitational waves generated by two colliding black holes nearly 1.3 billion light-years away. This was also the first direct evidence of the existence of black holes.

≥ A FITTING END ≤

Stephen Hawking, who had not expected to survive to thirty after being diagnosed with ALS, managed to live a full and happy life, dying at the age of seventy-six. He died "peacefully," according to his family, at his home in Cambridge on March 14, 2018. When the news was announced, prominent figures from around the world in science, entertainment, and politics sent heartfelt tributes, and the flag of his Cambridge college flew at half-mast. Among the guests at his funeral were actors Eddie Redmayne and Felicity Jones, Queen guitarist and astrophysicist Brian May, and astronaut Tim Peake.

A service of thanksgiving was held in Westminster Abbey in June 2018, and his ashes were interred near the graves of Sir Isaac Newton and Charles Darwin. Stephen's most famous equation—the one that shows that black holes emit radiation—was inscribed on his memorial stone. His words, set to music, were beamed into space from a satellite station in Spain toward the nearest black hole, known as 1A 0620-00. It was estimated they would arrive in the year 5475—the first-ever human contact with a black hole.

CONCLUSION

ASKING THE BIG QUESTIONS

Stephen Hawking was one of the most important and celebrated scientists of our age. He made extraordinary breakthroughs in cosmology and constantly challenged the world of physics with his ideas, theories, and predictions. His book *A Brief History of Time* gave millions of people access to the latest theories and discoveries about the universe.

Not just a scientist, Stephen became a global celebrity with a world-famous computerized voice. His opinion was constantly being sought by the media on all manner of subjects, including time travel, the possibility of alien life, and the dangers of robots. People were attracted to his wisdom and sense of humor and marveled at what he had managed to accomplish while living with such a severe physical disability.

ACHIEVEMENTS IN SCIENCE

Stephen made many contributions to the science of cosmology. Here are some of the main ones:

SINGULARITIES AND THE BIG BANG

Stephen's groundbreaking work with Roger Penrose in the 1960s helped show that singularities—infinitely small points that contain infinite mass and gravity—could exist in nature, and he theorized that our universe could have begun with a singularity.

HAWKING RADIATION

This was Stephen's crowning scientific achievement. In 1974, he overturned the scientific consensus that nothing could escape a black hole, by showing that black holes emit radiation. In so doing, he also showed that, over time, black holes can shrink and ultimately evaporate.

THE INFORMATION PARADOX

Stephen's discovery of Hawking radiation led him to a worrying realization, which he revealed in 1981: if black holes can evaporate, what happens to the information they swallowed? If it is lost, that would break a fundamental law of quantum mechanics. His announcement ignited a debate that continues to this day.

$$S = \frac{Akc^3}{2\hbar G}$$

COSMIC INFLATION

Alan Guth's theory of cosmic inflation (that the very early universe underwent a brief period of rapid expansion) is now widely accepted. But it might have failed were it not for Stephen's important work in 1982, when he showed how quantum fluctuations during the inflation period gave rise to the later formation of galaxies.

HARTLE-HAWKING STATE

In 1983, Stephen and James Hartle published a new model of the big bang, known as the Hartle-Hawking state, or no-boundary proposal. In this, they showed that in the very early history of the universe, time did not exist in the sense that we know it. Therefore, the universe could not be said to have a beginning. The Hartle-Hawking state remains one of the most important theories about the initial state of the universe.

$$S = \frac{Akc^3}{2hG}$$

TOP-DOWN COSMOLOGY

In 2006, Stephen, along with Thomas Hertog, proposed a theory they called top-down cosmology. They suggested that the universe didn't have one unique initial state, but consisted of a so-called "superposition" of every possible initial state. Thus, it is the present state of the universe that determines its initial state, not the other way around.

Stephen Hawking was working at the outer reaches of human understanding about the cosmos. Many of his theories are currently untestable by experiment and may never be testable. It could be that his ultimate legacy, and the truth of his claims, won't be known for decades or even centuries. Perhaps his biggest single achievement isn't the discoveries he made but the questions he asked, and where those questions have led us.

> "We remember Newton for answers. We remember Hawking for questions. And Hawking's questions themselves keep on giving, generating breakthroughs decades later. When ultimately we master the quantum gravity laws, and fully comprehend the birth of our universe, it will be by standing on the shoulders of Hawking."
> —Kip Thorne, 2018

NOT AFRAID TO BE WRONG

Stephen Hawking wasn't always right. In fact, he was quite often wrong. And that's hardly surprising with someone so unafraid to propose profound new ideas that challenge traditional ways of thinking.

Stephen was groundbreaking not only in his science but also in his way of *doing* science. Unlike many scientists, he was a natural showman. His love of making bets, for example, naturally drew the interest of the press and public. And what's more, he didn't mind being proved wrong. In fact, he almost seemed to relish it, sometimes conceding bets before either his supporters or opponents expected him to. The point for Stephen wasn't winning or losing a bet; it was the debate itself, and what new ideas might grow from it.

> "[Stephen's] a searcher, he is looking for things. And if sometimes he may talk nonsense, well, don't we all? The point is, people must think, they must go on thinking, they must try to extend the boundaries of knowledge."
> —Isobel Hawking (Stephen's mother), in *Stephen Hawking: An Unfettered Mind* (2012)

PROOF OF HAWKING RADIATION

In August 2018, in a laboratory in Rehovot, Israel, a team of scientists carried out a landmark experiment. They re-created the effect of a black hole in their laboratory, and they observed it emit radiation.

The scientists didn't create an actual black hole in their laboratory. That would have been highly dangerous and, anyway, beyond the capabilities of current technology. Instead, they re-created the *effect* of a black hole by sending laser pulses through an optical fiber—a glass fiber as thin as a hair. The pulses interfered with each other, producing a region within which light waves couldn't escape, a bit like a black hole. Importantly, this experiment provided real-world confirmation of Stephen Hawking's discovery. As the team leader Ulf Leonhardt said:

Hawking radiation ... can happen whenever event horizons are made.

First Observation of the Hawking Radiation

BLACK HOLES DON'T SUCK

STEPHEN HAWKING WAS RIGHT!

Stephen had died in March of that year, so he just missed out on witnessing the experiment that proved him right. Had he been alive, he might even have won the Nobel Prize for Physics, which is only awarded to living people who have had their theories verified by experiment. But, as Hawking himself said:

> "No one undertakes research in physics with the intention of winning a prize. It is the joy of discovering something no one knew before."

AN INSPIRATIONAL FIGURE

That Stephen Hawking managed to achieve all he did as a scientist and author while enduring an ever-worsening disability makes him a truly inspirational figure. As his disease progressed and his ability to move and communicate declined, it would have been very easy to give up. But he did the opposite: he worked even harder, developing new methods of working, and adopting cutting-edge technologies to overcome his physical limitations.

He defied all predictions made at the time of his diagnosis, living on for decades after doctors had given him just a few years. On several occasions, he faced life-threatening medical emergencies, yet through it all he continued to work, travel, and lead an active, fulfilling life. But Stephen never wanted to be defined by his disability. He thought of himself as a scientist first and foremost, and, thanks to his extraordinary discoveries, that is how he will be remembered.

"Look up at the stars and not down at your feet. Try to make sense of what you see, and wonder about what makes the universe exist. Be curious."
—Stephen Hawking

 # Timeline

January 8
Stephen Hawking is born.

Cosmologists George Gamow and Ralph Alpher suggest that the universe could have started with an explosion.

1942   1948

British astronomers Hermann Bondi, Thomas Gold, and Fred Hoyle propose the steady state theory.

January
Stephen is diagnosed with ALS.

American astronomers Arno Penzias and Robert Wilson discover cosmic microwave background radiation (CMBR), offering strong evidence to support the big bang theory.

1963   1964

Dutch astronomer Maarten Schmidt discovers quasars, suggesting the existence of black holes.

The term *black hole* first appears in print, in an article by journalist Ann Ewing.

Fred Hoyle coins the phrase *big bang* to describe Gamow and Alpher's theory.

October
Stephen begins his graduate work at Trinity Hall, Cambridge.

1950   1959   1962

October
Stephen begins studying natural science at University College, Oxford.

March
Stephen completes his PhD.

Astronomers Louise Webster, Paul Murdin, and Charles Bolton suggest that Cygnus X-1 may be a black hole.

1966   1972

Stephen, James Bardeen, and Brandon Carter propose four laws of black hole mechanics.

February
Stephen publishes his discovery of what would come to be called Hawking radiation.

Stephen is appointed Lucasian Professor of Mathematics at Cambridge University.

1974   1978   1979

American astronomers Vera Rubin and Kent Ford confirm the existence of dark matter.

Astronomers at the Max Planck Institute in Germany provide evidence for a supermassive black hole at the center of the Milky Way galaxy.

September 14
Scientists in the US detect gravitational waves for the first time, caused by the collision of two black holes.

2002   2014   2015

November
The Theory of Everything, a film about Stephen's life, is released.

1985

After catching pneumonia, Stephen undergoes a tracheotomy and loses the ability to speak.

1988

April
Stephen's book *A Brief History of Time* is published and quickly becomes an international bestseller.

Astrophysicists Saul Perlmutter and Brian Schmidt discover that the expansion of the universe is accelerating.

2018

March 14
Stephen Hawking dies.

August
Scientists in Israel prove the existence of Hawking radiation by re-creating the effect of a black hole in a laboratory.

2019

April
An international team of astronomers captures the first image of a black hole.

Further Reading

→ *A Black Hole Is Not a Hole* by Carolyn Cinami DeCristofano and Michael Carroll (Charlesbridge, 2017)

→ George's Secret Key series by Lucy and Stephen Hawking (Simon & Schuster)

→ *Stephen Hawking: Get to Know the Man Behind the Theory* (People You Should Know) by Cristina Oxtra (Capstone Press, 2020)

→ *Who Was Stephen Hawking?* by Jim Gigliotti (Penguin Workshop, 2019)

Websites

→ bbc.co.uk/bitesize/articles/zjkp8xs
Information about Stephen Hawking, including a video and a quiz.

→ science.nasa.gov/astrophysics/focus-areas/black-holes
A NASA website all about black holes. It includes videos, a chart, a timeline of recent discoveries, and other information.

Glossary

big bang theory: The theory that the universe began with the rapid expansion of matter from a state of extremely high density and temperature.

black hole: A region of space with a gravitational field so intense that no matter or energy can escape from it other than Hawking radiation.

civil service: The departments, agencies, and other bodies that administer a country and help the government carry out its policies.

cosmic inflation theory: The theory that the very early universe experienced a brief period of rapid expansion, then continued to expand less rapidly. This theory attempts to explain why CMBR is smooth and even, yet the present-day universe is "lumpy" with stars and galaxies.

Glossary

cosmic microwave background radiation (CMBR): A faint radiation that fills all of space. It is the oldest radiation in the universe, dating to around 380,000 years after the big bang, when it was cool enough for the first atoms to form.

cosmology: The branch of science that explores the origin, development, and history of the universe.

entropy: The amount of disorder or randomness in a system.

event horizon: The boundary around a black hole beyond which light or any other form of energy cannot escape.

galaxy: A system of millions or billions of stars, as well as gas and dust, held together by gravitational attraction.

Glossary

general relativity: The theory presented by Albert Einstein in 1915 that shows how gravity is a result of the warping of space and time (or space-time) by matter. The predictions of general relativity have been confirmed in all observations and experiments carried out to date.

gravity: The attraction between two objects that have mass, making them move toward each other.

information paradox: A puzzle relating to black holes and the fate of information (physical objects and their properties) that falls into them. Cosmologists have calculated that information could permanently disappear inside a black hole and that a black hole could shrink and ultimately disappear. This seems to contradict a core principle of modern physics: that information can be transformed into something else but never completely lost.

nuclear fuel: The hydrogen and helium that stars burn during their lifetimes.

Glossary

paradox: A seemingly absurd or contradictory statement or theory.

particle accelerator: A machine used for scientific research that accelerates subatomic particles, such as electrons or protons, to very high speeds. The particles can be aimed at a fixed target or be smashed into other particles. Detectors record and reveal new particles and radiation produced by these collisions.

photon: A particle of light.

physics: The branch of science concerned with the nature and properties of matter and energy.

quantum mechanics: The branch of science that deals with the motion and interactions of subatomic particles.

quasar: A vast and remote celestial object that emits extremely large amounts of energy. Quasars contain massive black holes and may be a stage in the development of some galaxies.

Glossary

radiation: The emission of radiation in the form of high-energy subatomic particles.

singularity: A point in space-time where matter is infinitely dense, such as at the center of a black hole.

steady state theory: The theory, now discredited, that the universe had no beginning. According to this theory, the universe maintains a constant average density because more matter is continuously being created to fill the void caused by the universe's expansion.

string theory: A theory that attempts to unite general relativity with quantum mechanics to create a theory of everything. It proposes that subatomic particles are, in fact, unimaginably tiny strings of vibrating energy.

subatomic particles: Fundamental particles much smaller than an atom, including electrons, neutrons, protons, and photons.

Glossary

theoretical: Concerned with the theory of a subject rather than its practical application.

thermodynamics: The branch of science that deals with the relations between heat and other forms of energy.

thesis: A long essay involving original research, written by a candidate for a university degree.

wormhole: A theoretical tunnel between two separate points in space-time. It is not known whether wormholes exist.

Index

A

Alpher, Richard, 152–153
ALS, 46–48, 90, 140, 152; *see also* disability

B

Bantam publishers, 88–89, 94; *see also* Guzzardi, Peter
Bardeen, James, 63, 153
Berman, Robert, 33–34, 40
Berry, Gordon, 29–30, 32–33, 39
big bang theory, 42, 44–45, 53, 80, 82, 84–86, 95, 126–127, 142–143, 152–153
black holes, 2–5, 8–9, 21, 59–63, 65–67, 69–72, 77, 79–81, 95, 102, 109, 116–117, 119–120, 127, 133, 138–140, 142–143, 147, 152–155
Bondi, Hermann, 45, 54, 152
Brief History of Time, A, 9, 95–96, 106, 122, 141, 155
Briefer History of Time, A, 122
Bryan, Richard, 29–30, 33, 39
Byron House School, 14

C

California, 70, 73, 92
Caltech, 70, 102, 109
Cambridge, England, 12, 73, 75, 91, 101, 140
 university, 27, 37, 40, 42–43, 45, 52, 54–55, 76, 132, 136, 140, 155
 University Press, 88, 95
Carr, Bernard, 58, 70, 114
Carter, Brandon, 63, 153
CERN, 89, 133; *see also* Large Hadron Collider
Christodoulou, Demetrios, 109
Clinton, Bill, 30
cosmic inflation, 143
cosmic microwave background radiation (CMBR), 44–45, 82, 127, 152
cosmology, 42–43, 87, 97, 109, 138, 141–143
cosmos, 5–6, 9, 126–127, 145
Cygnus X-1, 71, 102, 153

D

dark energy, 109, 154
disability, 9–10, 54, 56–58,

Index

76, 92, 99, 123, 129, 141, 149
Dorset, England, 17
Dublin, Ireland, 119–120

E
$E = mc^2$, 21, 66, 95; *see also* theory of general relativity
Earth, 3, 16, 41, 71, 128
Einstein, Albert, 5, 7, 20–21, 53, 60, 66–68, 80–81, 139; *see also* $E = mc^2$; theory of general relativity
electric wheelchair, 71, 73, 75, 77, 100, 108, 112, 133
England, 11, 20
entropy, 61–63
Equalizer, the, 92–93, 115
event horizon, 7, 59–60, 65, 80, 109, 117–118, 120, 123, 138–139, 147
expansion of the universe, 22–23, 42, 44–45, 53, 109–111, 155

F
Fella, Judy, 73

G
galaxy, 3, 23, 154
Galfard, Christophe, 115–116, 119
Galileo, 11
Gehrig, Lou, 46, 48; *see also* ALS
Geneva, Switzerland, 89–90
George's Secret Key to the Universe, 127
Germany, 11–13
Gold, Thomas, 45, 152
Grand Design, The, 126
Graves, Robert, 20
gravity, 3, 7–8, 68; *see also* singularity
Guth, Alan, 82, 143; *see also* cosmic inflation
Guzzardi, Peter, 94–95, 97

H
Hartle, James, 84–85, 110, 144
Hawking, Frank, 11–15, 17–19, 22, 26–27
Hawking, Isobel, 11–12, 14–15, 19, 22, 26, 127, 146
Hawking, Lucy, 57, 59, 70, 75, 87, 127–128, 137

Index

Hawking, Mary, 14–15, 17
Hawking, Philippa, 14–15, 17
Hawking, Robert, 57, 70
Hawking, Timothy, 57, 107
Hawking radiation, 65–66, 70, 77, 80, 116–117, 135, 142–143, 147, 154–155
Hertog, Thomas, 124–125, 127, 144; *see also* top-down cosmology
Higgs, Peter, 133–134
Higgs bosun particle, 133–134
Hoyle, Fred, 43–45, 52, 152–153; *see also* steady state theory
Hubble, Edwin, 23, 42; *see also* expansion of the universe

I

India, 26
inflation theory, 82–83
information paradox, 77–81, 116–117, 119, 138, 143
instanton, 110–111
Iran, 40, 42
Israel, 99, 147
Israel, Werner, 58

J

Jones, Felicity, 135, 140
Jones, Jonathan Hellyer, 75, 101

L

Laplace, Pierre-Simon, 81
Large Hadron Collider, 133–134
Lewis, C. S., 30
Linde, Andrei, 82–83, 111; *see also* inflation theory
London, England, 11, 13, 15, 17, 26, 46, 50, 58, 75, 134

M

Maldacena, Juan Martin, 117, 120
Mason, Elaine, 101, 113, 124
May, Brian, 140
Michell, John, 5
Mlodinow, Leonard, 122, 126
Morris, Errol, 106
Moscow, Russia, 82
Mozart, 58
My Brief History, 124

Index

N

Newton, Sir Isaac, 76, 140, 145
Nobel Prize, 134–135, 148
no-boundary proposal, 84–85, 110, 144

O

Oppenheimer, J. Robert, 8
Oxford, England, 11–12, 69
    university, 12, 27–32, 35–37, 39–40, 153

P

Page, Don, 73
Penrose, Roger, 53, 55, 61, 69, 99, 109, 114, 121
Perry, Malcolm, 138
photons, 60–61, 64
Powney, Derek, 29–30, 33–34, 39
Preskill, John, 109, 116, 120–121

Q

quantum mechanics, 63–65, 67–68, 78–79, 97, 116–118, 143

R

Redmayne, Eddie, 135–136, 140
Royal Society, 70, 75

S

San Francisco, 77
Schwarzchild, Karl, 7
Sciama, Dennis, 43, 54, 56, 69–70
Simpsons, The, 107–108
singularity, 8–9, 44, 53, 59, 85, 109–110, 118, 142
space exploration, 128–129
Spain, 19, 140
St. Albans, England, 17, 46, 49
    High School for Girls, 19
    school, 20, 22, 28
stars, 3–4, 7–8, 27, 45, 53, 59–60, 71, 82, 103, 127, 139
steady state theory, 42–45, 52, 152
Storminger, Andrew. 138
Suffolk, England, 51
Susskind, Leonard, 80, 114, 117, 120

Index

T

theory of everything, 67–68, 96, 133

Theory of Everything, The, 135–136, 154

theory of general relativity, 5, 21, 67–68, 80, 116, 118, 139

Thorne, Kip, 58, 70–72, 102, 104, 109, 116, 120–121, 145

time travel, 104–105, 131–132

top-down cosmology, 125, 127, 144

Traveling to Infinity: My Life with Stephen, 49, 135

Turok, Neil, 110, 112

U

universe, 2–3, 5, 9, 11, 16, 21–23, 42, 44–45, 52, 61–62, 66, 68, 79–82, 84–85, 87–89, 98, 102–105, 108–111, 114, 117, 120, 122, 124–127, 133–134, 139, 141–145, 152, 155; *see also* cosmos; galaxy

Universe in a Nutshell, The, 122

V

Virgin Galactic, 128

W

Westminster School, 22

Wheeler, John, 8, 70

Wilde, Jane, 49–51, 54–55, 58, 75, 90–91, 101, 124, 135–136

Wilson, Harold, 30

Wolf Prize in Physics, 99

Woltosz, Walt, 92; *see also* Equalizer, the

World War II, 11, 15

wormholes, 102–104

FOLLOW THE TRAIL!

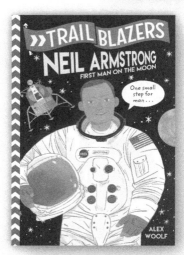

TURN THE PAGE FOR A SNEAK PEEK AT THESE TRAILBLAZERS BIOGRAPHIES!

Excerpt text copyright © 2020 by Sally J. Morgan.
Excerpt illustrations copyright © 2020 by Emma Trithart.
Cover art copyright © 2020 by Luisa Uribe.
Published in the United States by Random House Children's Books,
a division of Penguin Random House LLC, New York.

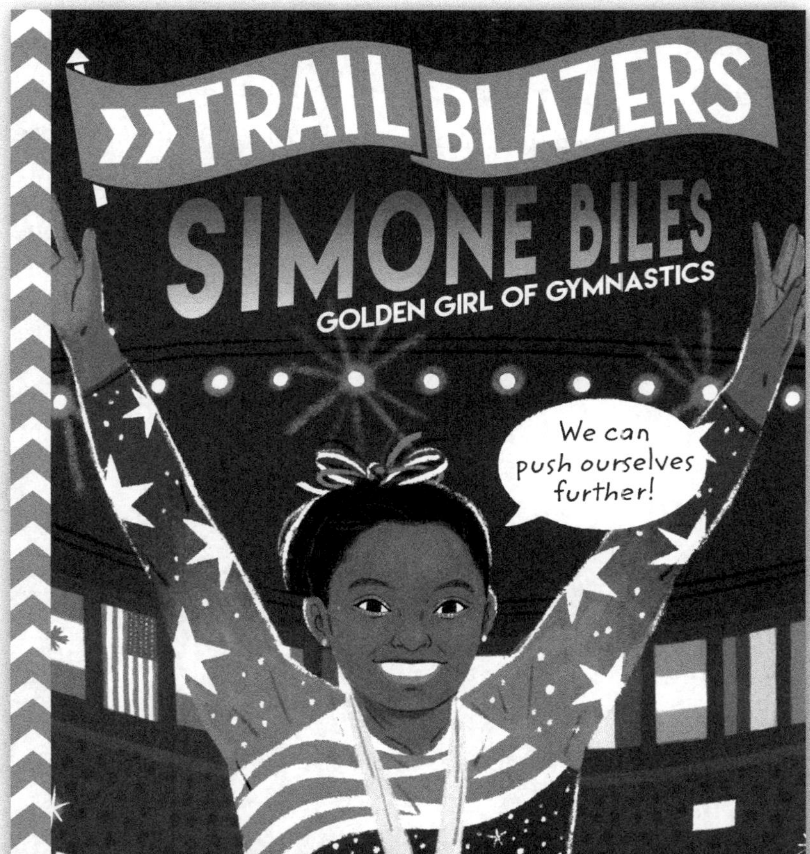
TRAIL BLAZERS
SIMONE BILES
GOLDEN GIRL OF GYMNASTICS
We can push ourselves further!
SALLY J. MORGAN

Inside Bannon's Gymnastix

Bannon's Gymnastix was the perfect place for a field trip. It was filled with trampolines and soft mats and had more than 20,000 square feet of space for the kids to explore. But while it might have looked like a playground to Simone

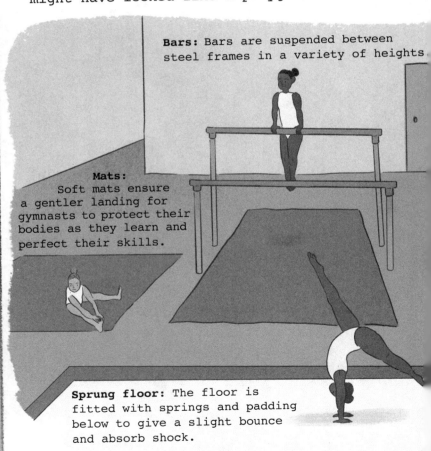

Bars: Bars are suspended between steel frames in a variety of heights

Mats: Soft mats ensure a gentler landing for gymnasts to protect their bodies as they learn and perfect their skills.

Sprung floor: The floor is fitted with springs and padding below to give a slight bounce and absorb shock.

and her friends, Bannon's was actually a world-class gymnastics facility, offering training not only to children taking their first steps on the mat, but to elite gymnasts ready to participate in national and international competitions.

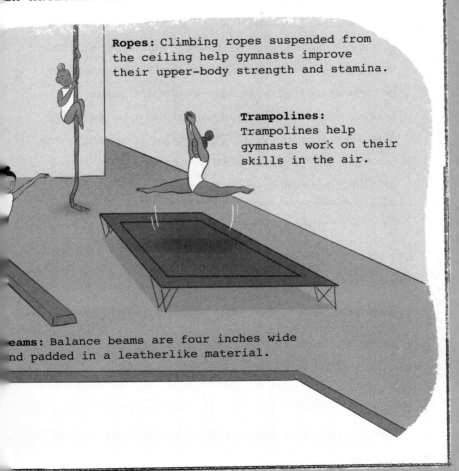

Ropes: Climbing ropes suspended from the ceiling help gymnasts improve their upper-body strength and stamina.

Trampolines: Trampolines help gymnasts work on their skills in the air.

Beams: Balance beams are four inches wide and padded in a leatherlike material.

> It's a moment I'll feel forever. . . . I'm excited about the whole team being together to start training.

There was a tradition for the women's artistic gymnastics team to give themselves a name. The 2012 Olympic team had called themselves the Fierce Five. Simone and the other girls agreed on the Final Five, both in honor of the fact that they would be the last team coached by Márta Károlyi, who had announced that she would retire after the games, and because they would be the last team of five to compete. The plan was that for the 2020 Olympic Games onward, teams for women's gymnastics would shrink to four, but starting in 2024, teams will have five gymnasts again.

The Final Five

Along with Simone Biles, these gymnasts made up the Final Five:

GABBY DOUGLAS (See page 72.)

LAURIE HERNANDEZ
Born: June 9, 2000
At 16 years old, Laurie was the youngest member of the Final Five. The 2016 Olympics was her first major international competition.
Star events: balance beam and an expressive floor routine

MADISON KOCIAN

Born: June 15, 1997

Madison won gold at the 2015 national championships on uneven bars and tied for first at the world championships in the same event. Madison was specially selected for the Olympics to give the team the best chance at achieving a medal in this event.

Star event: uneven bars

ALY RAISMAN (See page 73.)

Simone had qualified for the team in first place, but a stumble on beam showed she still had work to do if she wanted to be sure of gold. She would have to improve quickly—they were due to fly to Rio in just sixteen days.

Excerpt text copyright © 2020 by Paul Virr.
Excerpt illustrations copyright © 2020 by Artful Doodlers.
Cover art copyright © 2020 by Luisa Uribe.
Published in the United States by Random House Children's Books,
a division of Penguin Random House LLC, New York.

»TRAIL BLAZERS

ALBERT EINSTEIN
THE GREATEST MIND IN PHYSICS

Imagination is more important than knowledge.

PAUL VIRR

What Is Light?

For centuries, scientists had argued about what light actually was. When you heat an iron poker, some of the heat energy is turned into light. As the poker gets hotter, it glows red, orange, and then white. German physicist Max Planck was interested in how energy, temperature, and the color of heated objects are related. He discovered that energy doesn't flow steadily but is transferred in specific packets, each of which is called a quantum (plural: quanta).

Max couldn't figure out why. That was where Albert came in.

Albert explained how the specific colors produced by hot objects are due to light acting as a stream of particles. Each particle or quantum of light carries a specific packet of energy. The higher the frequency of the light, the bigger the packet of energy. Each frequency corresponds to a different color.

The Famous Equation

As if special relativity wasn't enough to make 1905 a year of scientific miracles, Albert finished by writing a short paper about energy and mass. In this almost casual postscript to special relativity, Albert noted how energy and mass are essentially the same—they can be converted into each other. This brief afterthought included the first version of the now-famous equation:

$$E = mc^2$$

E is energy, *m* is mass,
and *c* is the speed of light.

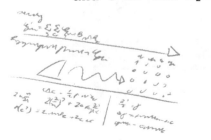

Albert's equation revealed how vast amounts of energy could be released from tiny amounts of matter. He had just described the source of the nuclear power that lights up the stars.

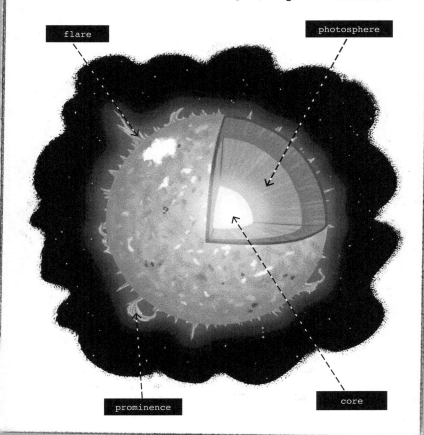

Excerpt text copyright © 2019 by Alex Woolf.
Excerpt illustrations copyright © 2019 by Artful Doodlers.
Cover art copyright © 2019 by Luisa Uribe and George Ermos.
Published in the United States by Random House Children's Books,
a division of Penguin Random House LLC, New York.

»TRAIL BLAZERS
NEIL ARMSTRONG
FIRST MAN ON THE MOON

One small step for man...

ALEX WOOLF

⋛ FLYING LESSONS ⋛

Airplanes remained Neil's first love. His dream was to become both a pilot and an aeronautical engineer—someone who designs and builds planes. About three or four miles outside Wapakoneta was Port Koneta Airport. Neil cycled or hitchhiked there as often as he could to watch the planes land and take off, and talk to the pilots.

When he was fifteen, Neil began saving up for flying lessons. He got a job at Rhine and Brading's Pharmacy, where he earned forty cents an hour. A one-hour flying lesson cost nine dollars, so he had to work twenty-two and a half hours to pay for one lesson! Neil supplemented his earnings at the pharmacy by offering to wash down the airplanes at Port Koneta. He even helped the airport mechanics with some routine maintenance work, servicing the planes' cylinders, pistons, and valves.

Eventually, Neil had saved up enough money to pay for some lessons. A veteran army pilot named Aubrey Knudegard taught him. They flew in a light, high-wing monoplane called an Aeronca Champion.

Aircraft Fact File

Name:	Aeronca Champion
Nickname:	"Champ"
Length:	21.5 ft. (6.6 m)
Wingspan:	35.2 ft. (10.7 m)
Engine:	65 horsepower
Top speed:	100 mph (161 kmh)
First flight:	April 29, 1944

COMING SOON . . .

Martin Luther King Jr.

J. K. Rowling

Amelia Earhart

Lin-Manuel Miranda